SOME COWS ARE ON THE PITCH...

THEY THINK IT'S ALL OVER...

it is now!

An extraordinary account of a year inside African football

SOME COWS ARE ON THE PITCH...

THEY THINK IT'S ALL OVER...

it is now!

An extraordinary account of a year inside African football

Iffy Onoura with **Graham Clutton**

This edition published in Great Britain in 2013 by DB Publishing, an imprint of JMD Media.

ISBN 9781780912332

Printed and bound by Copytech (UK) Limited, Peterborough.

Contents

PROLOGUE

I'm a second generation British-born, of Nigerian parents, and never slow to bore my own children with, "the world today is a very different one from when I grew up".

However, not-withstanding some ugly pockets of racism that inevitably rear their head in times of economic downturn, the rights that mine and the previous generation fought for, are now enshrined in British culture. And they're here to stay.

But where does that leave that lineage from Africa, the continent of our parents? Well, for me, my consciousness was re-awakened back in Ghana in 2008, when I found myself in the capital, Accra scouting for my new employers Blackburn Rovers. Like the other scouts on duty in Accra at the time, we were there to report on the best of the available emerging talent, at the continent's showpiece tournament. I don't recall passing on any gems other than the likes of Drogba and Toure, who were already familiar to Europe's footballing elite. However, I do recall returning home with a renewed desire to spend time in Africa in the future.

I'd been seduced by the raw spirit and joy of the fans and the resourcefulness of the people. Rather like any great boxer, there's a moment in your life when you take stock and look for your own place in history, no matter how big or small. Well, my own was big and having visited Africa very infrequently in the past, the attraction of the Motherland to me was seductive. A seed had definitely been planted within.

However, it's one thing having that dream, it's quite another seeing it realised. Never could I imagine that only a couple of years later, I'd be heading back to that continent, with all my hopes and dreams tied up in endless possibilities as coach to the Ethiopian national team!! I was asked by many of my friends; 'Why Ethiopia?' I couldn't tell them for sure, all I could say was that it was too good an opportunity to pass up. Never mind why, WHY NOT, I thought? It almost felt that a final piece of a jigsaw was being put in place, as all my footballing narrative up to now, had been played out just to bring me to this point in my life. Heady with ambition and daring, I saw myself as some kind of nomadic traveller coach: part Dr Livingstone, part Pep Guardiola, a man for all seasons with his eyes on the prize of World Cup 2014 in Brazil, and a whole lot in between.

CHAPTER ONE

Back to my roots

It had all started so innocuously, one moment arriving at Premier League Headquarters in Lancaster Gate, to meet, in the words of an agent friend of mine, "an important man from the Ethiopian Football Federation". It turned out to be the President, Mr Sahlu. Soon, we are discussing the country, its football and the Federation's desire to appoint an English coach to cement relations with the Premier League, and it's Chairman Sir David Richards. The relationship had begun some years before. The fact that my parentage is African undoubtedly helped and it's only a whirlwind two weeks, including a whistle stop weekend in Addis Ababa, before I'm boarding a plane, being met by my assigned driver and beginning a new life in Addis Ababa as the unheard of coach from England.

The press conference to herald my arrival, is held at the Sheraton hotel, which is soon to be my new home. It's an underwhelming affair played out to a

clearly sceptical media. However, I'm unconcerned, suffice to say I'm here now and I've got to hit the ground running as the games aren't too far away. I can only see the possibilities: the country hasn't qualified for the African Cup of Nations for over 30 years and has yet to qualify for a single World Cup. Even allowing for the endemic poverty here, for a country of some 80 million, the second most popu-lated country in Africa, it's an under-achievement needing a challenge from a professional enthusiast.

Luckily for me, I've always been a planner, enjoying the strategy and the grand design over the minutiae, and I can see the challenges, pitfalls and poten-tial ahead. Also, a coaching career spent playing the straight man to a variety of larger-than-life managers has prepared me for life in the fast line.

Paul Merson, Andy King and my very close friend Peter Jackson are endear-ing characters, to a man, and never mind any measurable success in manage-ment, each possesses a latent brilliance of sorts and an intuitive knowledge of football and players.

Me? Well, I'm more complex, I'm a different kind of beast, sustained only by a largely unwavering belief in my abilities, despite it must be said, only scant ev-idence of them. Nonetheless, my time has seemingly come and a mix of pride and defiance is urging me not to return to England until I've left a mark. For now, I'm literally on my own and it's a giant leap into the unknown.

Here goes....................

MONDAY JULY 5TH

The overnight flight from Heathrow is smooth and I'm met by my driver Wand-wsan (Wandy) and the Head of Media at the Ethiopian Football Federation, Melaku. It's been less than a week since I was here on a fact finding mission and it's nice to see their friendly faces. A short drive later and I'm checking into the Sheraton, Addis Ababa's magnificently appointed 5 Star Hotel. Set back on a hillside, it looks imposingly down on the sprawling metropolis below, home to nearly 4 million people as they go about their daily lives. I won't lack for ameni-ties here, that's for sure.

I'm pretty tired though and take the opportunity to have a quick nap before I'm up, changed and sitting down with the President (Sahlu). He informs me of some less than great news. On my last visit, I attended a game between two of the top club sides in Ethiopia. The teams would supply the bulk of the national side, or at least that was the plan. Unfortunately, in my absence, they had met again, this time in the cup. The league winners, Saint George, had contrived to get FIVE men sent off; of which two would be serving two-year bans for assaulting the referee. Oops. Now, we're hardly Spain as it is, but imagine Vicente del Bosque without David Villa and Andres Iniesta and you'd be getting close to the full aftermath of that game. Later that day news comes through that the Nigerian president has just lost a first-to-blink-loses contest with FIFA over government interference in football. This means they will now be in our qualifying group for the African Cup of Nations. My job has just been made that bit harder. Cheers!

TUESDAY JULY 6TH

I wake up and force myself to the gym. The Sheraton doesn't have one, so I'm in the hands of Wandy. He doesn't actually train himself, but proves himself very handy in negotiating a five-day pass for me at a new gymnasium in town. I clamber on the treadmill, ready to undertake my usual session, but two minutes into the session, and I'm in serious trouble. I've failed to factor in the altitude, so I'm puffing like Thomas the Tank Engine and unable to carry on. It's a painful lesson learnt!

Later that day, we go off to the national stadium where the pitch is sodden with all the recent rain. It's distinctly unplayable which is a shame as I was hoping to hold my first session on that particular surface. Not a chance now so it's plan B. We are going to head off to the training camp facilities in Nazret about 100km from Addis and appreciably drier.

Having been spoilt by the staff at the Sheraton, it's an immediate voyage of discovery, a trip into the unknown. Not only am I out of my comfort zone, but I'm faced with the almost impossible task of sorting out 44 players that I've never met. "Chigarrellem", as they say here, ("no problem"!). I return to the hotel and can't get my Skype working to speak to the kids and my partner Nadia. I content myself with watching Netherlands beat Uruguay 3-2 to reach the World Cup Final and try to sleep whilst the hotel band strikes up right outside my window!

WEDNESDAY JULY 7TH

My worst fears are confirmed. We arrive at the hotel at Nazret, after a two hour white knuckle ride courtesy of Wandy, who it transpires, is hostile to all road users….everywhere! The hotel is hardly the Sheraton and as I soon discover it's not got the requested internet, nor on closer inspection, a working power socket. It's not the worst hotel I've ever stayed in, but it's not far off.

Unfortunately, things don't improve when I finally greet the players. There are 44, as I thought, but it's a party somewhat imbalanced in composition. Stood in front of me are five goalkeepers (so far so good), just three centre halves (aaah, problems ahead), 11 left backs (are you kidding me?), three central midfielders (just three eh?), two right backs (well, they pick themselves I guess!), five wide players (whatever!) and 15 strikers (where's my coat?).

It's our first meeting and feeling like a little Englander, I talk in broken English with an assistant/translator which dilutes my Churchilian rhetoric somewhat. As I retire to my room, later in the day, to watch Spain beat Germany 1-0 to reach the World Cup Final, on a grainy TV, under a mosquito net, with one eye open, I reflect that for the first time since I began my African adventure, I seem to have mislaid my mojo!

THURSDAY JULY 8TH

I wake up determined to mentally re-group and to roll with it all. It wasn't to last. I went to see the "pitch" we were using for training, only to discover that it's a cow field with no markings. The irony of travelling two hours with Wandy, to a place lacking comfortable accommodation and a pitch no better than the one we left in Addis, did occur to me as I silently wept inside. However, I rallied and we located the "groundsman", who by hand, no less, marked the pitch with white lime scale. They're nothing if not resourceful around here. The players played their part too, contesting a lively 11 v 11, replicated in the afternoon as we somehow worked the 11 left backs into the four teams, without too much rancour.

After a long day of relative triumph over adversity, I took Wandy for a couple of well-earned beers and to chew the fat. I'm already quite fond of Wandy. He's a good guy and he told me more about his family life and how his wife was living in the USA. Whilst it was nice to open up, I had a feeling that he rather liked his beer. Mindful of his driving on the way down and the glazing of his eyes, I thought it best not to extend our session beyond the regulation couple.

On our return to the hotel, I was informed that there were five more players arriving in the morning, including, I kid you not, our 12th left back. I wept again!

FRIDAY JULY 9th

After a long morning and the onset of the midday sun, I decided this Englishman (technically a Scot, but work with me here!), would give the players the afternoon off. After lunch, Wandy and I go for a drive, ending up in a pleasant village called Sodere, which has an outdoor swimming pool. On the way Wandy truly reveals himself (not literally, of course). On busy roads lined with people, due to the absence of proper pavements, he's officially a truly crazed man. Simply put, Wandy doesn't believe that anyone else should be on the road except him. He refuses to cross the centre line in the road, preferring instead to toot his horn and practically drive at whatever person, animal or mineral, has the misfortune to be in his line of vision. When I suggest that this is generally what I've come to understand as, ATTEMPTED MURDER, he merely shrugs and protests that it's "his" road. This morning I swear he tooted his horn at a blind lady being helped by another lady across the road. Worse is, I feel complicit in his madness, now shifting uncomfortably in the seat at every toot. What makes it worse is that he's so deferential to me, it's beyond humbling. Every morning he drives the 100 metres to my hotel, to pick me up. Resistance is futile; despite my best pleadings he insists and does the same every evening too. In fact they're all at it here. I can't pick up a bag, cone, etc, without someone taking it off me in an instant. I mentioned it, in a phone call to Nadia later that night, suggesting that it may be a policy she could adopt when I return to England. A long silent pause ensued, suggesting it wasn't an opinion she seemed to care for much!

SATURDAY JULY 10TH

I'm a bit of a control freak by nature, but even I'm desperate to delegate some of the coaching duties. Unfortunately, I simply can't as my assistant is not a coach. He speaks reasonable English and acts as my translator, but that's about it. Needs must and I organise some small-sided games and pray the cream rises to the top at some point. After all, outside of the obvious handful, I'm struggling. In the afternoon, we head off to another facility which we can use next week and while it's certainly a better set up, pitch maintenance as everywhere, is something of an afterthought.

This seems like a test of not only my resolve, but other qualities of patience, compromise and flexibility. When I think of it, they are all things I know I can improve on in general, so why not here and now?

SUNDAY JULY 11TH

Well, it's officially judgement day as I have to wield the axe and cut the squad down to a more manageable 25. I affect an air of dispassionate professionalism, but the truth is that I'm more than a little concerned, not least because of potentially missing someone. Let's face it, I only know a few names and faces. This could be a disaster. In the end it's not too bad as I hitch up my trousers and do my best Simon-Cowell impression and duly crush the hopes and dreams of no fewer than 20 players. Ouch! Still, the dirty deed is done. To be honest, I'm thankful to be on the road back to Addis and the comfort of the Sheraton. I greet it like a long lost friend, promising to stick about now, until at least the day after tomorrow! I watch Spain deservedly beat an aggressive Dutch side, to lift the World Cup and it's actually a great fillip for me. I can point to the fact that similar to ourselves, Spain aren't a physically big side, but still dominate games through the simple means of dominating possession of the football. Inspired, I go to bed dreaming of Iniesta and Xavi, as Ethiopians!

MONDAY JULY 12TH

We've made tentative plans to be in the Federation first thing, for no other reason than to look like we're efficient. Predictably the gesture is wasted and as no-one seems to have noticed we're back from camp (did they even notice we'd gone I wonder?). I head off to the hospital to get my jabs. Initially, the place doesn't entirely fill me with confidence, looking as it does, like a hut at the end of a dirt track. However, a wizened lady jabs me surprisingly gently in both arms and now I'm ready to take on the best that Ethiopia can hit me with – and for 10 years to boot!

Unfortunately, what the jabs can't seem to combat is a famously sensitive constitution. Apologies for the mental image, but I could be crapping through the eye of the needle right now. And it's not pleasant!

TUESDAY JULY 13TH

So, it's day two of my abortive mission to the Federation, but this time I've hatched a cunning plan. I called a meeting on the pretext of letting them have some feedback on the training camp and selection process. If the truth be known, the meeting was called in a bid to chase up all my earlier requests which they'd hitherto nodded at sympathetically, but pretty much ignored. Eventually, we leave for Nazret again, at 4pm, some six hours after we'd got to the Federation and just in time for an evening meal, which I can't indulge in fully. That said, it could be a blessing in disguise as I was never sure about the food at the Adama where the players and staff are staying. That's the staff except Yours Truly, who mindful of the place they put me in last week, had done his homework and located a pleasant establishment, more in keeping with the style to which he's become acquainted.

Now, in England, everyone from the players through to the backroom 0staff would complain if I stayed 4 star and they didn't, but here, unless I 'm very much mistaken, it's not only accepted, it's expected!

WEDNESDAY JULY 14TH

First day of proper camp, and wouldn't you just know it. After whittling the number down to 25, more players have been sent, swelling the number to 29. Oh, and by the way, the goalkeeping coach from last week has gone home and has no phone for people to contact him. Why didn't they just send the players last week, I think to myself? This was meant to work with the ones selected. It was not meant to be an open camp to Tom, Dick and their best friend, Harry. However, coaching is nothing if not being adaptable and after a tough morning and afternoon session, I reckon it's gone well today. So much so that I suggest a couple of beers to Wandy, knowing full well he's never refused one, ever! We cruise around and find a decent bar attached to a hotel and the beer's cheap! Around 12 Ethiopian Birr gets you a very pleasant bottle of St George. Now, with the exchange rate roughly 25Birr to one English pound, I'll allow you to do the math and calculate how cheaply you can get drunk here! I head back to the room a little later to be confronted with further evidence that all's still not well and I'll have to continue my soup, fruit, and, er, beer diet, for another day at least.

THURSDAY JULY 15TH

Another day, another number of players to train. Unknown to me, until I've finished carefully planning my session, one player has had to leave camp for reasons as yet unidentified. I suppose you've just got to go roll with it all for now and then pick your moment to set out your rules. It doesn't help that I can't really bounce my ideas off anyone, so it's going to be a lonely road ahead.

FRIDAY JULY 16TH

Long day today and I'm seriously tired by the end. Another player has cried off and I joined in at times, to even things up. My assistant/translator, Atnafu is nominally meant to be in charge of the players and their hotel, so later that evening when I see some players casually leaving the hotel after I'd issued fairly strict guidelines, I realise that I'm now on the horns of a dilemma. Do I hit them hard or turn a blind eye so long as they train well? After all, I know I'd have been bored senseless in their shoes. Hmmm, I'll sleep on it.

SATURDAY JULY 17TH

Wake up musing about what to do with the players, but decide to hold counsel till after the practice game. We decide to take our travelling camp to Wonje, about half an hour away. The facility is actually quite decent (Hooray). I play what I consider to be the strongest team against another, almost daring the players to under-perform. They don't. In fact over the 90 minutes it's an unmistakeably, good standard. Unfortunately, whatever thoughts I had are quickly overtaken by the Great Lawnmower Crisis. The pitch at Wonje required cutting and we had to arrange for the mower to be transported from the Federation in Addis. So far, so good you'd think. Now, we needed that same mower to cut the grass at where we've been training at Adama. There then ensued a sort of Mexican stand-off between the driver, who wanted money to make the extra trip and a rapidly unravelling Atnafu, who was responsible for the whole operation. Conducted in mostly Ahmaric, I decided to opt out of this and leave them to it.

SUNDAY JULY 18TH

A long day's travel to Sotchmande lies in store, to watch a game in the company of the president, Sahlu. I think he's come away from Addis for a change of scenery and wants to meet up for a progress report. It's a long drive and I'm knackered by the end of it. Wandy and I leave after breakfast and it's dark before we return. In between, the game is a tad dull, not helped by taking place on a very poor pitch, surrounded by a shale running track. I slip off early to see the rather more impressive, Hallie resort, named after the great athlete, Hallie Gabriel Selassie. As luck would have it, the Great Man is there and introductions are made via Wandy, as he wishes me good luck in my job.

He must know something I don't, as on our return to Adama, Atnafu rings to give me the news about the missing players who've failed to report back on time as promised. In the circumstances, I'm grateful for the presence of Dr Elias who's arrived from Addis to help with fitness training for the players. He's a super-fit 50 something, with plenty of views about the current state of Ethiopian football. He may be a good man to have at my side.

MONDAY JULY 19TH

I arrive at the hotel to find that Atnafu has told the players to be on the bus for 8.30am, despite the fact that every day prior, it's been 9.30am. I take him to one side and explain that he's got to start listening to the instructions or there'll be a raft of problems ahead. I play it firm but fair with him, and for the rest of the day, he reins himself in admirably.

It soon becomes clear that he's not the only issue I've got to address. I spot two of the players leaving the hotel later that evening having specifically been told not to. It's clear my credibility is on the line. I've been reluctant up to now, to over-crack the whip, but this is a step too far. I know tomorrow demands a restoration of authority otherwise this whole adventure could well unravel. There's clearly an issue of discipline here and though I remind myself that English players are hardly angels, in these regards, this has the feel of the most significant moment thus far. Staff and players alike are awaiting my response and I can't shirk it, even if I wished to. The climate here is one where discipline is everything and it's expected to be administered from on high, no excuses!

TUESDAY JULY 20TH

A potentially defining day, even this early in the adventure. I spoke to the players this morning, invoking my best Churchillian rhetoric, as I laid down the law. It's always a high-risk strategy challenging players directly to toe the line or leave. What if they decide to leave? Who takes the rap then? Can Ethiopia withstand the loss of any players of any pedigree? Amidst the admirable qualities of adherence to team ethics and discipline, there's a balance of being pragmatic too and you forget that at your peril.

Training was conducted in the morning almost exclusively in the driving rain, as the heavens opened biblical style on Nazret. Just as well I'd prepared a plan B because Plan A, a speed and endurance session with Dr Elias, had to be shelved. The Doc is a steely but somewhat eccentric character, taken to perform his martial arts moves against imaginary opponents in full view of us training on the opposite side of the pitch. However, he's such a generous character, forever bestowing words of advice. He's been more of a mentor these last two days and I'm grateful for his presence.

WEDNESDAY JULY 21ST

Another day and more monsoon-like rain. To think we de-camped to Addis for this too! The Doc works the boys hard in the morning and I take them in the afternoon for a light session. Leaving aside his driving, I'm developing a good bond with Wandy. He's personable, astute and a good judge of people. I may be biased, but it seems to me he's wasted as a driver. He's never fawning to me, but understands he's there to serve, yet his views on life and particularly his occasionally wicked sense of humour, is perfectly in tune with mine. A good guy!

THURSDAY JULY 22ND

Decided, perhaps a little unwisely, to ring Sahlu about the money to take the guys out on Sunday, before later regretting my tendency, nay inability, just to keep my head down and get on with stuff. After all, I could be back in Bristol, so why don't I just take this opportunity, not ruffle any feathers and do the job? Because I'm so obsessed about doing something completely and utterly right, that's why. I need the day out on Sunday as much as the players. In truth,

I can already see how things are going to shape up -me being left on my own to somehow get the team into the African Cup of Nations come what may. It looks like a taller order than even I realised at the outset, but I'll give it my best shot.

FRIDAY JULY 23RD

I get up with a touch of training fatigue, but I'm quickly enthused by the session which goes well. A little too sure of myself, I head for the buffet at my hotel and don't hold back, which unfortunately means that I suffer badly later on. This time I can only blame myself for the long dark night that soon ensues. I can't take this for the next year I'll be half the man I was before I came out. I'm still struggling when the man from the Federation arrives unexpectedly and is surprisingly sweet and accommodating of all my previous requests. I manage politeness for as long as possible before heading back to resume hostilities with my intestines!

SATURDAY JULY 24TH

X Factor time again, as it's the day when I have to trim the squad back down to 25. Given that not one of the additions has really stood out, I'm not sure how much has been gained from the last 10 days in respect of new players. Still, I'll reserve judgement until after this morning's game. And my, oh my, what a shocker it is! What concerns me most is that the game is played out in front of the president. The players look leggy and lethargic. I can do no more than shake my head from the stand and let the sorry hour and a half play out. There is, however, the shining light of the hitherto unremarkable Tasfeye Alebechew, who amidst it all looked composed and authoritative as a holding central midfielder. He's one of the few six footers in the squad, so his performance is a welcome bonus. It's well timed too, as that position has always been one I've been quick to employ and in size and strength, he fits the bill perfectly.

When I later reflect on the game as a whole, it confirms what many coaches would admit that in defeat or in this case disappointment, you learn more about your team and squad than you do in triumph. I return to the hotel, only for events to take an Ealing comedy-esque turn. Ready for bed and clad only in my boxer shorts, I hear a commotion outside my door. After a little disturbance the night before, I make a beeline for the corridor. Unfortunately, I over-look the fact that due to the heat, I had previously opened the patio door. Cue door slamming behind me. Suddenly, I'm in the corridor near-naked and its Carry On bloody Hotel, circa 1974! I give it a minute or so and weigh up my options. Do I knock on a fellow guest's door? Noooooooo! Should I perhaps wait for a sympathetic staff member on patrols perhaps? Better, only none of them seem to be around, unlike every other day. I take steps gingerly down two flights, to be greeted by.....a friendly staff member from downstairs who mer-cifully puts me out of my misery by using the master-key. My room and bed, rarely felt as good as they did tonight!

SUNDAY JULY 25TH

Not the greatest of days today! My plan to take the guys off base to an outdoor swimming pool, was washed out and the day felt generally lifeless as for the first time I struggled with boredom and a little home sickness. It didn't help that my old dependable friend the Internet was down at the hotel too. Not a day to savour!

CHAPTER TWO

There are Cows on the pitch

MONDAY JULY 26TH

A rare sight as I woke up today, the sunshine was out for the first time in a few days. It's too late to save this leg of the training camp though as I'm determined to shift base. The pitches here are of poor standard and I honestly believe that a change of scene would be beneficial to us all. Not that it's that easy. I send an e-mail to the president just to facilitate the move and book accommodation etc, but not at all convinced that it will be straightforward.

TUESDAY JULY 27TH

Atnafu comes into his element today. After our talk the other day, I reckoned on things being a lot better so, when he answers my morning plea for a training pitch later that afternoon with a calm announcement that we could take the guys out to a village he knows, I'm obviously pleased. He assures me the pitch is good and what's more the players could relax and take a coffee afterwards.

It all sounded great, so we headed off with a spring in our step. We get to the "village", which

Appears initially to consist of a single horse and no coffee bar, nor for that measure does it appear to host a pitch, the whole point if you recall of our being there. I begin to fear the worst as we left the car to walk through dense forest, for what seemed an interminable time. Eventually we reached a clearing with a picturesque vista and a vast mountain backdrop and...... the "pitch". Now, Atnafu is perhaps 20 metres ahead of me at this stage, in conversation with the "manager" of the Pitch. He walks from one side of the Pitch to the other, across the centre circle and barely breaks stride throughout, whilst I stand transfixed at the scene in front of me.

Atnafu appears to be deep in conversation on the far side of the Pitch, whilst I'm surrounded by a posse of locals, all keen to know whether the Pitch would be suitable. As I glanced in turn from them to the Pitch and back again, I seriously wondered whether I was in an episode of Punk'd with Ashton Kutcher and whether soon from the undergrowth would emerge a hidden camera.

When it became clear this wasn't the case, I compose myself and affecting an air of regret, turned Down their "generous offer", and tried to compose myself. At that moment (always the WRONG moment, it seemed), Atnafu arrived back and scanning my face for clues, sought my thoughts. The following conversation ensued:

Atnafu: "So Coach, what do you think?"

Me: "Hmm, let me see, what do YOU think, Atnafu?" (There may have been a clue in my tone).

Atnafu: "Maybe it's not so great?

Me: "Not so great? Well, let's look at the evidence shall we?" (I felt as though I was David Frost on Through the Keyhole). "The pitch has a gradient of perhaps 1:10 from corner to corner, so clearly we'd be looking at the proverbial game of two halves. Also, I can confidently state that it's not been troubled by any such thing as GRASS for the last 10 years. But, and here's the thing, possibly the biggest single impediment to us using the pitch now, as I see it Atnafu, would almost certainly be that HERD of cattle in the middle of the centre circle, shitting away like their very lives depend on it!"

Wandy? To the car!!

It's a quiet journey back; Atnafu gets in the back of the car with me, seemingly unperturbed by the waste of the whole day and proceeds to read the paper like he's the CEO being driven to a leisurely lunch date, by his two lackeys!

WEDNESDAY JULY 28TH

Happy birthday me! I wake up to messages from family and friends, most remarking on the fact that I'll be celebrating it somewhere very different from in the past. The significance isn't lost on me as I head back to Addis in a bid to sort out a great many things about which I'm unhappy. The meeting doesn't go well. It's not that I don't get my point across to the president and general secretary; in fact I all but let them know exactly where their shortcomings have been and what needs sorting out. No. The problem is, as I learn later, that despite their constant nodding and promise to get on the case immediately, they aren't football people in any way and in many instances, simply don't have a clue as to what I'm talking about. They are also too proud to admit it. For instance I've mentioned the importance of scouting our opponents, Guinea, in their game against Mali two weeks today. THREE times the general secretary asks me what date is the game, despite it having been on the FIFA website for several weeks. I suspect the FIFA website isn't high on the search engines at the Federation office!

It's all in all, a thoroughly depressing day as the reality of the job begins to bite. They say it's lonely at the top, but this is beyond loneliness. Only the Technical Director, John Tesem and the common sense Wandy, can be classed as allies. For the first time, I seriously wonder what I've let myself in for.

THURSDAY JULY 29TH

Early start on the road back to Nazret for morning training. Atnafu rings up to check on our progress. I'll have to speak to him at some point, because his name featured high on my list of complaints yesterday. I give the guys a hard session today, but I'm a little awkward in front of them. They're probably the people who will decide my fate as I can't see anything other than continued clashes with the Federation for the remainder of my time here. It's only the support of the players that will keep me going psychologically and perhaps materially. Thankfully, they're a delight to work with today and training goes well.

John rings from Addis and fortunately, he's picking up the mess left to him by others re the still-unconfirmed friendly match. He also asks me to confirm the date of that game again (see yesterday). I almost weep in frustration. Atnafu is a bit quieter today, perhaps taking in yesterday's pitch fiasco. I actually do feel a little sorry for him as he's got no previous coaching experience. I was told he was an administrator at one of the clubs and a friend of the president and general secretary. They did ask me yesterday how he was getting on and I had to be honest and say that I felt he was struggling in the role. I resolve not to ask or expect too much of him on the training field, but with off pitch matters, he could despite the pitch fiasco the other day, be very useful.

FRIDAY JULY 30TH

Oh dear, Groundhog Day with Atnafu! The presence of a guy from the radio in Addis has brought out the worst in him as emboldened he marches off to the training ground, to play the Big Man, and move the kids off the pitch. Never mind that they're harmless and always play ahead of us using the pitch, today he wants to show off a bit. I'm not best pleased and tell him directly, this is becoming exhausting.

After training he wants to speak again to me. He's got genuine family issues involving a sick daughter and needs to go back to Addis to sort things out. Wandy's going off to Awassa early tomorrow, so it's not ideal, but I would always make allowances where families are concerned. Back at my hotel, I reflect once more on the loneliness of my current predicament after an animated conversation on the phone with the Federation, who still haven't secured a Friendly fixture. So, in summary: no friendly, no arrangements in place to scout the Mali v Guinea game and a high maintenance assistant. Oh, and I haven't been paid this month either!

SATURDAY JULY 31ST

We play an 11v11 game amongst ourselves and it's not too bad until I have to intervene due to a mid-game bout of fisticuffs between two of the players. I send the other 20 down the pitch whilst I speak to them both. I sometimes forget that they're all from different clubs and may have some individual rivalries. The game is otherwise important in clarifying a few other issues regarding selection. I do enjoy the responsibility of making decisions, but this is the national team after all, what I could do with now is the sagely advice of a trusted assistant to consult. Ah!

Wandy leaves early for Awassa on a pre-arranged jaunt and after the game Atnafu heads off too. My driver is now the taciturn physio, Isak, who actually lets cars out in traffic and refrains from running people over. How strange!

John from the Federation drops by to see us and gives us some money for our stay in Awassa. He's one of the few who's on top of things, but I had been concerned that whilst urging me to rebel, he'd been content to keep out of the crossfire. Thankfully he seems to have come around a little and talks of having heated discussions with increasingly fractious members of the Federation. I feel like the lightning rod for a lot of built-up tension in the Federation amongst various factions and my head's spinning. Oh, and by the way, I still haven't been paid!

SUNDAY AUGUST 1ST

We stop at a beach resort on the way back to Awassa where we're shifting base to. I thought it would be good for the players to go and relax after a good week's training and I managed to get money for it through the Federation. So, naturally I'm disappointed when the players are decidedly under-whelmed, and duly mope about. Bit of a faux pas on my part, I shouldn't have just presumed they would enjoy it, next time I'll let them decide their own leisure time

We arrive at the hotel to find that it's ok, and I check into my room. Predictably enough, one look at the pitch confirms it's neither suitable nor prepared, cue the call back to the Federation, I bet they're sick of me already. However, this isn't the end of the drama. It transpires that the players aren't in the first hotel we saw that was decent, they're in another and it's not decent! So, soon we're checking out and into another. Finally, and much later, we're settled, dispersed over three hotels for the night, entirely in keeping with the week just gone.

MONDAY AUGUST 2ND

The training pitch is a long expanse of land with a rusty goal at either end. What's more, the grass would comfortably conceal a lolling lioness and her cubs! I head to the very splendid Hallie resort, locate the gym there and secure its use for the guys, leaving Atnafu to sort out someone to cut the grass for training that afternoon. When we return later that afternoon, just the 18 yard box of one half has been cut, although to be fair someone has taken the trouble to put up the nets in both goals. So, I rip up plan A and revert to plan B which is a session based on the use of a penalty box and 25 players. It's a fun session actually and goes well so no harm done in the end. And that's the job lot of a coach in many respects, to improvise depending on numbers, facilities etc. I think I'll have to get used to that a lot here!

WEDNESDAY AUGUST 3RD

Today an initially innocuous phone call from the president to me, went down a road marked, "don't go there", which unfortunately we went right down, free-wheeling, with no brakes applied! The Federation as the governing body, is responsible for many of the things that should be in place i.e. hotels and facilities. Clearly no one seems to take any responsibility for it. I detail all this in my frustration and at the end of a breathless five minute phone semi-rant, I hung up wondering whether that was entirely smart of me, or whether I'd pushed my luck a little too far. However, at that moment there was little by way of facilities, no boots for the players, no fixture arranged AND I haven't been paid. It's inevitable that your well of patience would eventually run dry. Mine was arid!

Of equal significance is my relationship with Nadia. She's been studying really hard recently on her dissertation and the plan was for her to come out and join me later in the year. It seems a good time as any to make a quick trip home to see her and help with the move out of our rented place.

I did worry about the momentum on the team and the effect of my absence, but in truth that was all going to change in the absence of any friendly fixture now anyway. I told the players who, hard to read as ever, appeared to take it all with a resigned shrug, breaking only in to applause when I mentioned that their tracksuits, boots etc, were on their way.

After an unsure start I felt we were making progress and the discipline of the group had improved appreciably. I worried whether Atnafu would be able to cope without me there. I left him with a loose schedule, but I'm not hopeful in truth. He couldn't be more out of his depth had he been wearing goggles and a snorkel! I confirm my booking later that day on the overnight flight back to Heathrow, perfectly timed to coincide with the end of the heat wave of the last four weeks in England!

WEDNESDAY AUGUST 4TH

Well, this is a good start! Nadia's car has been clamped in Bath (yes, tax discs are required here sweetheart!) and so I'm stuck at Heathrow some two hours after landing. Eventually she shows and it's great to see her. She looks tired and stressed, but I'm really pleased to be back.

THURSDAY AUGUST 5TH

First proper day back and its nice. True, I'm concerned about the players enough to ring Atnafu to check that they've trained ok today, but I'm looking forward to seeing everybody here. And the day's idyllic too. Head to Bristol, pick up the kids and soon we're eating sushi in town and catching up on all the news.

With time now to reflect on my first month in the job, I recognise that I needed this break as much as anyone. The frustration was starting to overwhelm me and another few days over there might have sent me over the edge. From here it's easier to develop perspective and talking to the family makes it easier to put everything in to context.

FRIDAY AUGUST 6TH

Another day that I'm looking forward to, I'm off down to Plymouth to see my eldest daughter. She had a few health issues earlier this year, so it's great to see her looking so well and ready to finish her final year at university in October. We don't do much, just chill and go and visit her cousins, but it's those simple pleasures that I'm enjoying the most about being back.

After resuming battle with the M5, it's nonetheless a long day before I'm back in Bath around nine o'clock. It's moving day tomorrow which I seem to do every six months these days.

SATURDAY AUGUST 7TH

It's our last day in Bath and as we go past the university playing fields, I drool longingly at the grass (cut and lined), goals (with nets) and pitches (no cows!). After Ethiopia, I'll never take those things for granted again. We conclude an occasionally fractious day and it's late when we settle down for our last meal as residents of Bath. I've definitely fallen for the city and it's somewhere I'd love to settle down one day. For now though it's back to Bristol.

SUNDAY AUGUST 8TH

Sunday morning in Bristol soon becomes an exercise in purgatory as I attempt to get to London to see my family. However, it's not to be, the good citizens of Buckinghamshire are having a car-smashing jamboree on the M4 and my progress is suitably slow, limping into North London some three and a half hours later at 4pm. Good to see everyone, my sis and two brothers and spouses/fiancées/nephews etc. Get there in time to take up our Liverpool/Everton rivalry and catch Man Utd beating Chelsea, 3-1 in the Community Shield.

I return back to Bristol, already pining for the challenge of Ethiopia. Everything that's happened so far seems from this distance, no big deal all of a sudden and I realise how much I'm actually enjoying the job, frustrations and all.

MONDAY AUGUST 9TH

So many things to pay for and so little money, mean that I'm now bored and when I'm bored, I'm irritable. I'm just awaiting the call from David my agent, re the money and to confirm my return flight to Addis. No word from anyone in Addis. It's unnervingly silent.

TUESDAY AUGUST 10TH

I finally hear from people back in Addis, that a fixture has been arranged next Wednesday versus Kenya. It'll be short-ish notice as I'm not due back until the weekend before, but it's a GAME at last. Better news, at least. I realise that I've got to be more patient now, I've wanted to move too fast and I've got to rein myself in a bit. After some upheaval in recent times, many of the Federation are finding their feet and in my haste I've not appreciated that enough. Chill out a little, I tell myself.

WEDNESDAY AUGUST 11TH

Guinea already have the look of the team to beat in our qualifying group, impressively beating Mali 2-0 in a friendly match in Bermarko. Despite Nigeria's current troubles with FIFA, they too will be strong and our group suddenly looks from this vantage point, the proverbial Group of Death! I can't lose that first game against Guinea if I can help it, so it's more food for thought in terms of selection, tactics etc.

THURSDAY AUGUST 12TH

Wages arrive!!!!! I embark on a frenzy of spending at Ikea to furnish my very bare-looking Bristol flat which my son is moving into as house-sitter while he studies theatre at Bristol Old Vic. Nadia is due to move in too, but she too has a flat in Bristol which she's in right now. I don't even have time to assemble it, as I'm due to fly back in a few hours and there's still plenty to do.

FRIDAY AUGUST 13TH

I ring to confirm my flight details, only to be told that the flight is now full and I'll have to travel tomorrow afternoon instead. As frustrating as it is initially, I realise later it gives me the chance to finish things off properly here. So, it's another date with Mr Ikea, a welcome opportunity to say my goodbyes to the kids again (not as bad as last time thankfully, I was worse than them!) and then off to mate Mark's place in Windsor, close to Heathrow. I did have other stuff to do, but it'll have to wait until tomorrow morning.

CHAPTER THREE

The heat is on

SATURDAY AUGUST 14TH

What should be a routine 20 minute journey from Windsor to Heathrow is, in my world, fraught with the dangers of missing the flight. So, I've to meet my agent David near Paddington station to pick up the Tactics Board I've ordered online but had to send to David's place for him to bring to the station, and a Chelsea shirt for Wandy. Now, Dave's a lovely guy but ALWAYS late and I'm very anal about being late, so it's a relief when I'm finally at the airport, a couple of hours before flight time.

When we're called to board, the plane stays on the tarmac for nearly two hours due to bad weather. Of course my connection in Cairo, involves a two hour wait. It's entirely predictable that I miss it! Earlier it was also entirely predictable that, out of a family comprising mother and three kids sat in the row in front, where two of the kids were lovely and pleasant and one had borderline ADHD, the latter would sit directly in front of me. When she wasn't standing on the chair staring at me, she was rocking backwards and forwards violently while all along her mother slept!

Finally arrived back in Addis at around 9am local time, to be greeted by the familiar friendly face of Wandy. He was overwhelmed by his Chelsea shirt! I checked into the Sheraton, resisting the temptation to sleep as I was training the guys in a few hours and thought I'd probably feel worse if I did. It was nice seeing the guys and I deliberately greeted them warmly. Training is good, the artificial surface is better than what I'd remembered and it's nice to know my enthusiasm remains undimmed and if anything, re-kindled.

MONDAY AUGUST 16TH

My first full day back and from a coaching viewpoint, it's a rare (I think!) failure. Mindful of the game on Tuesday, I decide to focus on defensive work and shape, but it's a tough session to manage on your own and it soon becomes clear that in my absence some of the discipline, previously instilled, has slipped. The players are a little bored with something as structured as this. Even back in England most players would be happy to just play small sided games every day. I'm a big fan too. However, you do need to do tactical work as well and work specific to one unit of the team, i.e. defending. It's a question of picking the right times to do it, that's all.

In the evening we all convene to eat at the players' hotel and unless I'm very much mistaken, Atnafu is sulking like a small child when John Tesema drops by. As Tech Director of the Federation and someone who's lived mostly in the USA, I can speak more easily with him. The language of football is much better too. Atnafu seems to know this and is, bizarrely, jealous. The rest of the meal consists of him challenging John on various aspects. Now, given that John has just come from painting the dressing rooms at the stadium which will host the game on Wednesday, he's picked the wrong target. In the circumstances John is the model of constraint, quietly restating what he can and can't do, whilst Atnafu doesn't listen and continues to pursue the blind alley of his argument, doggedly. I shake my head inwardly at the ridiculousness of it all. It's not a crime to be out of your depth, so long as you can listen and learn quickly. Sadly, on this occasion, he does neither.

Later, I watch the first half of a match in which Man Utd cruise to victory over Newcastle. I've something of a soft spot for Newcastle and their admirable manager Chris Hughton, who I know and like a lot. His son Chris was at Lincoln when I was assistant manager and is a lovely guy too. Chris has a tough job on there, I wish him well.

As for me, I'll sleep on the Atnafu problem. I've made a conscious effort since I returned to be patient with him and, in truth, he made more of a fool of himself than anyone else with his behaviour earlier. The trouble is, he's now a drain on my thoughts, more so than any of the players.

TUESDAY AUGUST 17TH

It's the day before the game and at the press conference, the media are in rest-less mood. I feel like Daniel in the lion's den and it even prompts me to chat to Atnafu and apologise if I've upset him in the past. I'm not entirely convinced that it's merited, but for the sake of harmony and a new chapter, I'm happy to do it. Also, I'm beginning to recognise a seriously low patience threshold in myself. I must address the problem, otherwise this adventure could turn into a nightmare.

WEDNESDAY AUGUST 18TH

The day of the game and I resolve (or do I really?) to chill out and head off to the gym, which usually helps. A good work out later and we go off to meet the Kenyan delegation at their hotel to discuss match formalities. It's the pre-game meeting where we sit around the table, introduce ourselves (team man-ager, coach, captain etc) and basically discuss what kit we're wearing and how many subs we have. The whole thing probably lasts no more than 10 minutes and merely covers all those things that are normally done in England an hour before kick off when team sheets are handed in.

Kick-off is 4pm, so we set off at 2.15. The omens aren't good when we get blocked in at the hotel and then get caught up in traffic. We arrive and it's great to see a crowd of around 25,000 plus at this difficult to access stadium. When the anthems start (after a typically fussy insistence, five minutes before kick-off, on inspecting kit and shirt numbers in the dressing room), it's a proud moment.

The game kicks off and we make a comfortable start, controlling possession as Kenya drop off to defend. Then disaster strikes; we give away an unnecessary free kick wide on the touchline. The next few seconds are the stuff of a coach's nightmare. They cross into the box, we go missing in defence, the keeper flaps and we're 1-0 down. The rest of the half follows a similar pattern as we press forward, superior in possession. Half time comes and as promised I change the team completely, bar one. Similar to the first half we control possession but are struggling to break down a well-organised Kenyan defence. Then disaster occurs once more. They receive a free kick 30 yards from goal, it's struck well enough but straight at keeper no. 2. Unfortunately, the keeper pops it up in the air, flaps and spills it, 2-0. To compound the misery, they score again from another poorly defended free kick and 3-0 it is, welcome to the job! I'm guessing from the reaction of the fans that my honeymoon is well and truly over. I'm not sure it's quite sunk in yet, as the optimist in me before the game was anticipating a victory. It's only afterwards that the pragmatist asserts that it's our FIRST game in well over a year and the Ethiopian season hasn't started yet. Kenya on the other hand, played last week and their league season is already two months in. It's a crumb of comfort. The support from the president and Atnafu after the game makes only the slightest dent in my overwhelming feeling of disappointment.

THURSDAY AUGUST 19TH

The morning after the night before, and still the overwhelming feeling is one of disappointment rather than disaster. In fact, from the moment I leave the hotel and someone sticks up their thumbs and says; "good luck, we still believe in you", today is actually one of the best days I've had in Ethiopia. Out of adversity, I've recognised both my own culpability and shortcomings and that of the team. Now, the acid test. How do we go forward from here.

FRIDAY AUGUST 20TH

I spend some time in the gym this morning and play a bit of basketball too. I'm quite pleased with myself since the game, so I'm initially a little weary when the players come to me in a small delegation to talk tactics. I might have been a little defensive once, but now I'm actually pleased about how much they obviously care about things to that extent. Besides, they make some valid points, which I'm happy to take on board.

I actually go to the cinema with them to watch a film in Amharic which I understand to be a kind of slapstick romantic comedy. I get the gist of it ok and the film is well-received by the audience. The announcer even finds time to tell the audience prior to the screening that the national team is present. We receive some warm applause, which is quite remarkable given Wednesday's defeat. Further proof if more proof were needed, of the warmth of the Ethiopian people and the kind of support we could tap into if we do well in our qualifying campaign.

SATURDAY AUGUST 21ST

I keep it light and bright this morning, I've been around football and football players long enough to know that you have to handle the mood very carefully, even a few days after a defeat, lest the "blame", game begins. I was intending giving them some time off and I can sense they're grateful for a chance to escape the confines of the hotel and go home for the day.

The one great bonus about being away from home is the ability to watch live Premiership football at 3pm on a Saturday! We watch Arsenal dismantle 10-man Blackpool 6-0. I felt sorry for the Blackpool manager Ian Holloway as he's a good guy and a true football man. With him at the helm, I think they'll be ok to survive this season.

SUNDAY AUGUST 22ND

The players have the day off and Wandy's moving house, so it's the first day I find myself bored and with time on my hands. I shuffle around the hotel unconvincingly, having tried and failed to watch a DVD I bought on the street. Serves me right as well, don't normally invest in dodgy DVD's but I was a little desperate. The comeuppance was mine!

Doctor Elias eventually comes over and spends the afternoon with me at the Sheraton and we put the world to right over lunch. The key to survival here is definitely patience and rolling with all possible eventualities. Right on cue, the president rings about a friendly game which was promised but now is in doubt. I make it clear how important it is and that they should do whatever they have to, to make it happen.

MONDAY AUGUST 23RD

It seems like my forceful approach from last night has paid off, as they confirm a friendly v Chad this Sunday. Apparently they had a rarely-convened meeting of the committee and made the decision at the meeting. Also, they approved Richard Hill, my old assistant and friend from Gillingham, to come over and help with our preparations for the Guinea game. The wheels turn very slowly here as I confirmed with Hilly last week, so I'm pleased it's been sorted.

Less satisfying is training this morning. It could be the day off or just Monday morning blues, but there's a lethargy today that I don't like. I suspect that one or two are starting to feel comfortable so a few phone calls later and we've reinforced the squad with two more additions. When they arrive that evening my spirits are lifted appreciably, a bit like when you sign a new player. Let's see if it has the desired effect tomorrow.

TUESDAY AUGUST 24TH

Bingo! Training is up a notch or two as the lethargy of yesterday is well and truly shaken off. Everything about the guys today is sharp and the game we finish with is at times ferociously contested. I've been told that I have to cut the squad down, principally because of costs at the hotel, but also I have to send an approved squad of 22, 10 days in advance of the Guinea game. I can see the logic of it, as I reckon there was a lot of dodgy stuff happening back in the day, with regards to players and their nationalities. However, it certainly doesn't help me and I find myself praying for a clean bill of health between now and the game. As far as trimming the squad is concerned, I have to be careful. I only cut back three guys who I know won't figure. Anyway, I would have told them after the Guinea game anyway. Twenty five is a more manageable number too.

The guys take the news with barely concealed disappointment, as I offer the platitudes and encouragement for the future. All three of them are among the nicest guys in the squad which doesn't make it easier. However, maybe that's why it's them sitting here as opposed to the others. They lack a little bit of an "edge" to their game, which I feel most truly good or great players have.

WEDNESDAY AUGUST 25TH

The next day after the 'Night of the Long Knives' and training is conspicuously sharper. It often happens. As much as the survivors feel for the guys, no-one wants to be next in line for the chop, so efforts are doubled all round. In the afternoon, I go to the Federation to check on the progress of Hillys' plane ticket. Nothing is ever simple here, so a mere two days before he's meant to arrive there's still no confirmation e-mail. However, I'm assured everything's been approved. Now, where have I heard that before??

I return to the hotel to find the hotel lobby busy with cabin crew, business types and the kind of single attractive females that tend to frequent an upmarket hotel lobby in any major city of the world. The staff at the hotel are lovely too and I'm starting to get to know a few of them. They are always asking about the progress of the team and wishing me well. Lovely people, lovely hotel, what more could I wish for?

FRIDAY AUGUST 27TH

I finish training and have planned a nice relaxing afternoon, confident that Hilly's flight has been sorted out. Wrong! Hilly sends me an exasperated text saying that he still hasn't heard anything and he won't travel unless he does. I wearily head back to the Federation to find out what's been going on. Thankfully, my ally, John, is there and we stand over the lady in the office while it's being sent. I feel sorry for her, it's an instruction she clearly hasn't been given before from the general secretary who's gone off to Sudan for a few days.

Finally, Hilly texts me to say it's all been sorted and I can finally relax. I'm not a big drinker back home, save for the odd glass or two of wine. But here my alcohol intake has risen sharply. I blame a combination of the cheapness, the boredom and the stress. In fact I don't know whether to bemoan it or salute it!

SATURDAY AUGUST 28TH

Early start this morning as Wandy and I head off to meet Hilly at the airport. His plane is on time and it's good to see a familiar face. It's his first time in Africa so it'll all be an eye-opener for him too. After a quick breakfast, we go to the training ground and I introduce Hilly to the guys. For the first time, I can properly prepare the starting line-up, whilst he looks after the rest. It's a welcome relief and a chance to relax, safe in the knowledge that he's here to help take the pressure off me.

We eat later and he settles in to what must be a very unfamiliar environment. We spend the evening with the players watching the first half of the Kenya game on DVD at their hotel, all the time now working on hearts and minds ahead of tomorrow's game.

SOME COWS ARE ON THE PITCH... THEY THINK IT'S ALL OVER... *it is now!*

CHAPTER FOUR

Between a rock and a hard place

SUNDAY AUGUST 29TH

The day of the game, and I leave Atnafu to attend the pre-game brief, in the morning, whilst I go to church. I ask him to text me if there are any problems. I confirm that I will be IN church between 10 and 11, so to avoid ringing at those times, unless it is absolutely essential. So, when later he rings me twice whilst I'm still in church, I'm concerned as to what possible problems there might have been. I wait until the end of the service and call him, obviously anticipating a problem. 'No problem.' he says. 'I attended the brief and there is nothing to report.' So why ring? I want to say something, but resist and hang up.

We head off to the game at 2pm and arrive at 2.30 to see a sizeable crowd already in the ground. The national stadium is both under water and not marked out, so we play the game at a new astro turf facility a few kilometres from the centre of Addis called the Abebe Bikila stadium, named after the great marathon runner of the 60's.

The contrast between that and the state of the art facilities back in the UK, couldn't be more stark. Essentially there's only one covered stand looking out over a pitch with a running track around it. An inspection of the changing rooms confirms they're basic at best. There's a stone floor, no lockers or pegs, just a handful of chairs and benches on which the players can hang their clothes.

However, that's the least of my worries. I go out to mark the warm up before the game and get a good cheer from the crowd. It gives me a good feeling, until

Hilly reports that he's seen their team and they're huge. Cheers Hilly, I thought. I didn't ask him over here to make me nervous and talk up the opposition, so, what's the matter with him???

I needn't have worried because in Hilly's own words, "the team are a credit to you." We run out 1-0 winners, when on another day it could have been four or five given the scoring opportunities spurned. There's a real feel-good factor as we leave the stadium and head back to the hotel.

MONDAY AUGUST 30TH

Thankfully, we saw fit to make it an afternoon training session today and a light one at that. I was delighted with their fitness levels yesterday so the next few days will all be about recovery for those who've played. For the others, it's good to have Richard around, so he can work them a bit harder. I detect a slight grievance from Atnafu, about Richard. I think he feels marginalised despite me assuring him, before Richard came out, of my intentions. Also, Richard is someone he could talk to and get some tips from. Richard's played the role of assistant to the likes of John Gregory and Brian Little, so for Atnafu, he could be really useful. However I'm not sure Atnafu quite sees it like that, he's a VERY complex man and I sense there could be trouble ahead..........

TUESDAY AUGUST 31st

I'm not sure my decision to hit the gym for 9am was much to Hilly's, liking, nor to my body's liking either, but I suffer through it and work with the boys when they arrive an hour later.

We finish in time for lunch and as we are leaving, I notice that Hilly is deep in conversation with Atnafu. He tells me later that he admonished him for disappearing whilst we were in the gym to do his own gym work, saying that a good assistant wouldn't do that. Now, Atnafu did actually ask me first, so I feel a little sorry for him on this score and I make a point of saying that it was ok and not to worry. However, later I overhear Atnafu making a comment to Hilly along the lines of what training we "should" be doing. Now, I have not only shown great patience with this guy, but I've also resisted the chance to bad mouth him to the Federation. On top of that, it's clear the players don't really see him as anything other than a translator. One or two of the ones who speak good English made me aware of one or two problems when I left for England too. Again I left it alone and chose not to confront him. Yet here he is criticising me to Hilly. If he'd pulled me aside earlier and made a suggestion, I would definitely have listened and taken it on board had it have been a good one. But this way? Well………

WEDNESDAY SEPTEMBER 1ST

I wake up and as we head for training, I'm aware that I'm not comfortable with the week so far. Hilly has helped as I hoped on the training ground, but off it, his arrival has, through no fault of his own, disturbed the equilibrium. He's done all that I would have asked for and more, so if it's anybody's fault, it's clearly mine. I decide to leave things for now and see how things pan out today. When the session is poorly delivered (my fault), the players train half-heartedly (my fault) and two balls go missing at the end, I tell all the staff in no uncertain terms that today hasn't been good enough. I know I'm angry at myself as much as anything because we've all dined out on last week's result. We have become complacent.

THURSDAY SEPTEMBER 2ND

The Day it All Came to a Head. So, training is bright as I take control a little more today and as we head off, I feel far happier for having done so. Back at the hotel the president and general secretary speak to the players about bonuses. Better to come directly from them rather than me and it's good for the players to know where the president's coming from. As I see them off into the night, I return to the lobby to see Atnafu in a heated argument with a journalist who'd come to observe. I attempt to calm things, only for Hilly and Atnafu then to argue in front of everybody. It's an ugly scene which I eventually manage to calm. Hilly duly apologises. Had things have stayed that way, I would have congratulated myself on my skilful handling of things. However, later on I try to get to the bottom of the whole thing with Atnafu, privately. It doesn't go well. Whether it's a build-up of tension on both our parts, I'm not sure. Still, I suppose, in hindsight, it has been coming. The discussion gets heated, as he starts shouting at me and jabbing his finger in my face. Before I know it, I've got my hands around his lapels on his jacket and then throat and we stumble, comedy style, over a table just off the lobby. It's all over in a flash and there's been no blows exchanged at all. The commotion alerted the hotel staff, who side with Atnafu. I know this isn't good.

The rest of the evening is a flurry of phone calls and damage limitation, but I know I shouldn't have grabbed him, despite the provocation. As I lie awake well into the early hours, I wonder if my adventure is all about to end - before it's really begun.

SATURDAY SEPTEMBER 4TH

The morning after and following more early phone calls, I head to the players' hotel and head to Atnafu's room to pursue a policy of mea culpa. He's complaining of a sore back from when we fell over the table, but gradually his stance softens and I resolve to come back and see him again after training. We all then convene at the training ground minus Atnafu and I make some excuses to the players who must all be aware of what happened, but seem virtually non-plussed. Training, thankfully, is bright again and we head back to the hotel. Atnafu and I head off to the Federation who seem keen to brush things under the carpet, thankfully, and I reflect, not only on a vital game in two days' time, but potentially an uncertain future after that.

SUNDAY SEPTEMBER 5TH

It seems that damage limitation is the order of the day and an uneasy compromise has been reached. So, by the day of the game, things appear to be ok. However, I'm not daft, I know people are biding their time until after the game to deal with everything. I try to remain as relaxed and calm as possible as we make plans for the match. However, any possibility of that is shattered, as having discussed the starting eleven amongst the staff before picking the team the day before, I then open up the discussion on who should be subs. Atnafu then decides this is the time to say that he doesn't agree with the team I've selected and Adane Girma should start. It should be a laughable situation, but I'm too "in the moment" now. I call him a "clown" gather my various bits of paper and head to the stadium perhaps not in the best frame of mind.

Arriving at the stadium, the atmosphere is electric and I receive a wonderful ovation from the fans as I put out the discs for the warm up. The stadium is nominally meant to hold about 25,000, but there's people hanging off flood-lights, walls etc. It's a real throwback to England, once upon a time and I get a real sense of the responsibility I have. The national anthem only adds to the occasion. It's a beautiful piece of music and the hairs on the back of my neck stand up.

The game itself is a wonderful experience. After an understandably nerv-ous start, we settle down and begin to dominate matters, playing football of the Gods in our new attacking 4-3-3 formation. However, we spurn numer-ous opportunities to score and I begin to think that our carelessness is going to come back and haunt us. When we finally do score after 20 minutes, there's bedlam in the stadium and joy unadulterated. The feeling and the noise from the crowd is so uplifting.

Unfortunately, events then conspire with a force I can only describe as Bib-lical. The ferocity of the rain that falls in the next 20 minutes is akin to being stood in the middle of a tornado! A mere "storm" doesn't do it justice, but now it's our team, short on physical stature, but high on technical quality, who appear frozen in its eye. As for the crowd in the open stand, well they are defi-nitely voting with their feet as they make a dash across the running track and down the side of the pitch, running for cover.

During the confusion our left back freezes in possession, can't recover and his mistake is punished. 1-1. The force of the hailstones and rain is such that the referee finally halts proceedings and the players leave the field. Despite the disappointment of conceding, I try to stay positive in the dressing room. We try to re-group and play resumes after a 10 minute break, but the game is a farce. Huge puddles on the pitch means the ball doesn't roll. It's enough to call the game off in England, but not here, not now. Inevitably it affects our passing game and we naively try to play through the puddles and concede a corner. All that you need now is a goalkeeping blunder, right? On cue, it comes. Our stat-uesque goalkeeper stays rooted to the spot whilst a Guinea player, from almost under the bar, heads the ball into the net. We are 2-1 down and immediately, it's half time. I admonish the players a little for their lack of nous, but I know deep down, it's called experience and we don't have enough of it in the team.

Soon it shows. I know I have to make changes early and bring on our two experienced, physical, strikers. I also know that we have to score early because

I'm sending out a message of intent and of course, we'll be more vulnerable defensively. And so it proves. After we get a corner we have FOUR clear chances to score as its pinball in the Guinea penalty box. Suddenly, they clear the ball up field, retrieve possession and within a matter of seconds, we are 3-1 down. Game over. A fourth goal, late on, conceded in similar circumstances to the third, seals our fate. I try to rally the troops afterwards and everyone urges positivity. After all, we've still made big strides of late and but for the intervention of the weather, who knows how the game would have panned out.

I'm subdued afterwards and the result is only half of it. I know there's trouble brewing with Atnafu, courtesy of the incident the other night. The man has, in mind at least, got me by the cojones! Hilly leaves on the evening flight and I curse him for heading off without me.

MONDAY SEPTEMBER 6TH

It's all strangely quiet, this morning, save for the urgings of the guys as we leave the hotel, to stay positive. I get a phone call from Atnafu to tell me that most of the players have left already. We were all meant to meet before leaving, so once again, the plans have changed! This is confirmed when of the seven players who did stay put, by the time I return an hour later, there are now only three. I bid them good holiday and head off, mentally to book mine. So, as long as the players are off, I'm heading out of this mad house too, and sharply.

TUESDAY SEPTEMBER 7TH

The first shot across the bow comes when David calls from London, saying he's had a conversation with Sahlu, the president. He informs me the subject of Atnafu has been raised. I draw a sharp intake of breath and listen intently before telling David exactly what's been going on. I'm told to prepare a report on the game from Sunday and a broader report on how I see things two months into the job. It doesn't take me long to do, but I'm then focused on going home. However, events conspire against me. First of all my money still hasn't cleared at the bank, so I'm unable to book my flight straight away. Then, as I'm about to execute plan B, I get a phone call requesting my attendance at a meeting of the executive committee, tomorrow. Despite my hollow protests I reluctantly agree. Another Night of the Long Knives ahead, it seems.

WEDNESDAY SEPTEMBER 8TH

A couple of early morning phone calls reassure me the nuclear option of me being sacked is unlikely to happen. Nonetheless, I'm more than a little nervous as we head into the committee room, of a central hotel in Addis. Not all are present, which I think is a blessing, but it still has the feel of a McCarthy-esque trial. I sit patiently as Atnafu has his say….for a full half an hour! Some of it is translated back to me in English, but it's not exactly reassuring to be in the midst of what amounts to a disciplinary hearing held in another language. I make my speech (I'm allowed less than two minutes!) which is a passionate and spirited defence of my role. In truth, I've got my eyes fixed on the prize of my flight home and right now, my main concern is being on that overnight flight. Finally, it's over and there seems to be a tentative plan for things to be resolved successfully. I say a few words to Atnafu to that effect.

Later, the president rings me confirming this. He also acknowledges the fact that the meeting was slanted in Atnafu's favour. I tell him that I understand, and genuinely do. My regard for him goes up appreciably. Whatever the rights and wrongs, he was in a very difficult position, having to balance the various interests involved. To that degree, he's done exceptionally well and I tip my hat to him. I think he's in my corner and I'm not sure how many others are here. Yep, this job just got a little more, lonely! If I could be bothered to think about it right now, I might be concerned, but all I can think of is going home to see my family and friends. I've never been more excited to see them.

THURSDAY SEPTEMBER 9TH

Arrive back to a rainy Heathrow, but I don't care at all. Instantly, I feel relaxed and it's a full FIVE minutes before I think of Atnafu or the Federation again. Mark picks me up and I'm soon heading back to Bristol. Not so fast though. All is not well on the M4 and it's five hours before I'm back home. Any other day and I would been gutted, but not today. I see the kids and all is good again.

FRIDAY SEPTEMBER 10TH

I sleep in and just spend the day relaxing and opening mail. I've got a busy weekend ahead of me so today's a proper chill day. It's late afternoon before I head out of the flat to pick up my daughter. She's still sleeping ahead of an early morning start to Liverpool to see friends and family.

SATURDAY SEPTEMBER 11TH

It's the anniversary of the plane hijacks in New York and all the news is dominated by a crackpot pastor in America who wants to burn a copy of the Qu'ran. I say 'let him and then let him watch over his shoulder for the rest of his days, with no police protection!' My daughter and I leave for Liverpool at 8am and we arrive at midday. Mind you, I did get a bit lucky en route: there was a Tranmere Rovers season ticket fan, who obviously didn't bear any grudges for my blink-and-you'll-miss-me-spell there. He was on the toll at the Mersey Tunnel as I arrived with just Ethiopian Birr for currency!

After that it's a race against time to say hello to all, before dashing off to see my boys, Everton, take on Man Utd at Goodison Park. It promises to be an extra spicy affair due to the proposed baiting of Wayne Rooney after his recent troubles. So, it's something of an anti-climax when it's revealed that he hasn't even travelled. Nonetheless, it's a great atmosphere and I'm grateful to Chris Hughton for getting me a ticket.

It's actually been a long time since I last went to a game at Goodison and I definitely wasn't sitting in the Director's box back then either. As smug as it's possible to be, I take my seat next to Everton legend Joe Royle and the rest of the club hierarchy. Joe (well, we're practically best friends now!), proceeds to give me a running commentary right through the game, mainly about the admittedly masterful performance from Paul Scholes. The game's something of a classic too, as the Blues lose a 1-0 lead and look dead and buried at 1-3. Cue an astonishing comeback as they pull a goal back in time added on, before equalising a minute later. Cue the celebrations as Yours Truly, Joe Royle, the chairman Bill Kenwright and Derek Hatton, the ex deputy council leader, all leap as one at the final whistle.

I get dropped off in town and pick up my daughter before heading off with her and two of my niece's to see my dad, their Granddad. He's not in the best of health these days, though his mind is still alert and I do feel guilty about leaving it for so long. Still, it's good to see him and we catch up over an hour or so. Then it's back to my brother's place, before heading up to Leeds (do keep up!) for my other brother's stag do. Me and my childhood mate, Mike, arrive in Leeds, minus accommodation and end up paying over the odds for a hotel room that screams "standard fare". Leeds is an old stomping ground, so we meet up with everyone and proceed to have a great night. It's been a good day. I haven't had too many of them recently.

SUNDAY SEPTEMBER 12TH

Wake up in somewhat less than rude health and take myself tenderly downstairs to meet an equally tender, Mike. As confirmed veterans, we head off early back down to Liverpool via Doncaster where Mike left his two German shepherd dogs last night. Whilst he's collecting them, Nadia calls. It's not been an easy time for both of us and things haven't been great. So, when she mentions about flying over to meet me in Addis, I'm a little taken aback. When she confirms her flight an hour later, I'm apprehensive. Unless things have changed dramatically between us, this smacks of trouble. I could do without this, I say, much to the amusement of Mike, who clearly finds the whole situation hilarious. Still, I put it to the back of my mind as we spend the rest of the day lazily chatting away in my brother's kitchen.

My daughter and I finally head off back to Bristol around three-ish, in time for her singing lesson. It doesn't get any easier saying goodbye to her, but tomorrow's already looking busy, so I have to go through the ordeal tonight. It's going to be a long six weeks until I'm back, so saying goodbye, is hard. I drop in to see my good friend Les Antoine ("Twon") that evening and he gives me the news that our friend and bronze medallist at the Sydney Olympics, Kath Merry, is expecting a baby. I'm really pleased for her as she's a great girl and was really keen to start a family. Mind you, it does seem weird her being pregnant. She's one of the guys is Kath and now she's going to be a mum. Well, I reckon she'll be a great mum and I'm actually quite excited for her.

MONDAY SEPTEMBER 13TH

I've a few things to sort out before heading off to Heathrow. I was going to travel late, but Nadia's arriving from Belgium at four o'clock where she's been visiting family, so I park up my car near the university and catch a train from Bristol to Slough, where Mr Reliable, Mark is picking me up and taking me to Heathrow. He drops me off and I wait for Nadia to arrive as she called earlier to say she was already here. I'm actually quite nervous about seeing her and when she finally arrives (she'd been at Terminal 1!) we embrace warmly, if a little awkwardly. Within the hour we'd had our first argument, oh dear, with an open return flight, this could be a long journey into hell!

CHAPTER FIVE

A triumph of will

TUESDAY SEPTEMBER 14TH

We land in Addis and it's good to see Wandy there to pick us up. I go to the Federation and find the pitch without any markings and the president and vice-president away until Friday. On top of that, half the players have yet to return from the break. Remarkably, the new stoical me takes it all in his stride. I even meet and greet Atnafu at the hotel, though it's clear there is still a little bit of awkwardness between us.

WEDNESDAY SEPTEMBER 15TH

Back at the hotel Nadia seems to be settling in ok and if we're not quite on the best of terms, she has at least made a few friends in the hotel. She's beautiful, intelligent and charming so it comes naturally to her. I think it helps that she's not quite familiar with the currency yet and is taken to giving out huge tips to the hotel staff, making her instantly popular with them!

THURSDAY SEPTEMBER 16Th

It's my eldest daughter's birthday, so I send her a text and call her later too. As for Nadia and I, we enjoy a lovely romantic meal in the French restaurant at the hotel and nearly get to the end of the meal without disagreement!

FRIDAY SEPTEMBER 17TH

A few more of the guys showed up today and training's bright, even allowing for the fact that Yours Truly makes up the numbers for the game at the end (winning team if you must ask!). I suffer for it though, as a long bath later and I'm fast asleep for an afternoon siesta. The rain is finally showing signs of abating and the sun is shining now in Addis, at last.

SATURDAY SEPTEMBER 18TH

All the guys are here now, bar two and it helps that things are cool between Atnafu and I. He surprises me as its genuine now and it may well be that the incident at the hotel got a lot of frustrations out in the open. It's a far better relationship already. Thank goodness for my break in England, it really gave me an opportunity to stand back and assess things. It is something I have always done. Just take a little time to step away from a situation and analyse exactly what is going on. I'm sure Atnafu has done something similar, possibly for the first time, so good on him for it!

SUNDAY SEPTEMBER 19TH

As one relationship starts to improve, another shows every sign of coming apart. It's a day off today and a day, in theory at least, to chill out and spend time with Nadia. The atmosphere's not great between us though and we stumble through uncertainly. This isn't going according to any loose plan we had and I'm conscious that, notwithstanding the improved relations between me and Atnafu, that I seem to be the common denominator in some inter-personal conflicts.

MONDAY SEPTEMBER 20TH

A little ahead of schedule, it seems that Nadia is ready to go back. It's been an uneasy time, but she's made up her mind to return to Bristol. As things haven't been great between us, I would have liked to have resolve things before she left. Sadly, it seems that's out of the question too. This looks terminal, past the point of no return, the flight's booked and she doesn't want me to even accompany her to the airport.

TUESDAY SEPTEMBER 21ST

I wake up having slept a little uneasily thinking about Nadia and hoping she's ok. I'll call a bit later, I decide. I even manage to have lunch with the players and staff at the hotel.

My day is actually quite productive and if there's still a nagging worry about Nadia, for now, I try to put it out of mind. So, it's actually a surprise when I answer the phone later and its Nadia calling from….. somewhere in Addis! Well, this is the worst possible news, particularly as she appears to be staying in a bed-sit somewhere. This is now my definition of Hell and I don't know where and when it will end. She hangs up without me knowing where she is.

WEDNESDAY SEPTEMBER 22ND

I can't let it go any longer, I've got to find her. She tells me where she's staying, but only because she's leaving that night. I get to her place in a less-than-exclusive area of the city and we finally talk properly, for hours. On the surface it's good, but as we go on it becomes clear that she's not getting on any plane tonight or, quite probably, any time in the near future. This confirms my worst fear about her coming over. Once she's here, it's entirely her choice when she goes back. I'm between a rock and a hard place: leave her there to fend for herself or take her back with me, despite the sure knowledge that we'll do this all over again. Wearily, I order a cab from reception to the Sheraton …for TWO! I don't know where this will end up, but I know it won't be a happy ending, that's for sure.

THURSDAY SEPTEMBER 23RD

Things are fine this morning, but we've been here before and I know that it simply it won't last. Nonetheless, I enjoy it while it does and besides, the guys are bright at training as we make a rare visit to the National Stadium to train on, wait for it, GRASS! I take the opportunity to train the guys hard today. However, there's mutiny in the air as basically they're fed up. They've not been paid in three months. Frankly, I don't blame them and wonder what else I might have done for them. Perhaps I've been focusing too much on other issues and have missed the bigger picture, namely these guys have trained for three months without pay and the novelty of me and our close relationship is no longer enough. Unhappy players, means unhappy football. I sense trouble!

FRIDAY SEPTEMBER 24TH

Days seem to be rolling into one now. I seem to be a skilled politician more so than a coach, forever spinning plates to keep everyone happy. I want the game with Madagascar to come as soon as possible and I want to give the players back to their clubs. The feeling might well be mutual now too, and again, I wouldn't blame them. After all, this last week or so has dragged and my words of advice/wisdom are starting to sound a little hollow, even to me. The doubts have set in and they're starting to take hold.

SATURDAY SEPTEMBER 25TH

We were meant to be playing a game today, but instead I opt for another session. Lo and behold after three months of injury-free bliss, the captain Samson pulls up with what looks like a muscular injury. This follows another injury, three days ago, which looked serious at the time, but not so now. Besides, Samson is the captain of the team and a true leader. We finish the session, but in truth it's another hammer blow in a week which has got steadily worse. Did I mention that I've already named my 18-man squad at the insistence of the Federation? No? Well, I have, so for 18, now read 16. Honestly, you couldn't make it up!

Nadia and I go to the museum in Addis in the afternoon. It's only small, but it gives a flavour of the rich history of Ethiopia and I make a mental note to visit some of the historical sites when I've time after the next game.

SUNDAY SEPTEMBER 26TH

We train today (Sunday) as it's a public holiday tomorrow and the players will have their day off then. We train early and the thorny subject of money raises its head again. I'm now like a fireman putting out fires everywhere, as I promise to take up the baton again next week.

The weather's picked up now, so back at the hotel, I take the opportunity to spend an afternoon by the hotel pool. Bliss!

MONDAY SEPTEMBER 27TH

I wake up determined to let it be NADIA day. Whatever she wants to do, I'll happily fall in to line. So, as we scour the streets for a pair of trainers for her to go the gym, on a public holiday when most of the shops are shut, I'm the very model of support. The entente cordiale, however, doesn't last the night though. She's been working hard on her dissertation and her tutor has asked that she amends it. I happily look over it and suggest a few changes, largely to do with the tone rather than the content. Unfortunately, it's enough to lead to another falling out!

TUESDAY SEPTEMBER 28TH

Nadia, to be fair to her, has spent her time here productively, spending some time with Sheik Alhamoundin, the billionaire owner of the Sheraton no less. Given that he bankrolls the Football Federation here, he's technically my boss! He's not often at the hotel, spending much of his time, until now, in Saudi Arabia. In fact it's rather like in Charlie's Angels, I've never actually met him! However, he's in town now and with their shared Arab background, he has clearly endeared her to him. Ethiopia is a country with a strong Arab influence historically and you can see that in the features of people here. I don't know enough about the hierarchy to pass judgement on any wider significance, other than when your partner is now on first name terms with the Sheik after a week, and you've yet to meet him, then effectively you're a long way back in second place of a two horse race!

WEDNESDAY SEPTEMBER 29TH

I channel my energies and efforts into training the guys and as ever, they train well enough to lift my spirits appreciably. However, there's more trouble brewing: the Federation have already asked me to name my 18 man squad for the trip to Madagascar and now they're refusing to call up our most important player, Fikru, because of the extra cost of bringing him over from South Africa where he plays his club football. I call the President and it seems to fall on deaf ears, even when I offer to pay for his flight myself. It's only when Atnafu speaks to the President that the matter is resolved satisfactorily and Fikru can be included in the party. Now, whilst I'm glad that Fikru's travelling, it does raise the question as to a certain shift in the balance of power. One thing I will definitely say is that despite everything else, Atnafu has never had another agenda other than the team being successful. He's definitely come up trumps here.

THURSDAY SEPTEMBER 30TH

It seems that Nadia's been spending most evenings now with the Sheik and his entourage networking and talking business possibilities. She excitedly tells me about some of the important people she's meeting and the potential opportunities arising from that. If it wasn't her whole reason for coming out here in the first place, then it could hardly have worked out better. I'm pleased for her as this is what we spoke loosely about when I was offered the job. Things are looking up.

FRIDAY OCTOBER 1ST

One of the players goes down in agony in training today, exposing the folly of reducing the squad so soon. Luckily, I haven't revealed the identity of the 18 to the players, so once again it's up to Atnafu to explain the latest turn of events to the Federation. They reluctantly sanction replacing him with another player. In some ways it might be to our advantage. Behailu who was injured is a lovely guy, but wouldn't have been a first choice anyway, more of a sop to Atnafu of whom he's a favourite. His replacement Mulugeta would be more of a useful squad member and more likely to be involved. At least the injury wasn't down to the pitch. Despite my best efforts, no work has been carried out at the national stadium pitch, so we've once again been training on the artificial surface. It's far from ideal as we've already had confirmation from Madagascar that the game there will be played on grass. Games are increasingly being played on astro-turf where possible in Africa due to the parlous state of some of the pitches there. But if we're playing the match on grass in Madagascar, then simply put, we need to train on grass!

SATURDAY OCTOBER 2ND

My plea for us to train on grass isn't met but this is the new phlegmatic me and I take it in my stride. The pitch is neither cut nor marked, so there you have it, end of discussion.

SUNDAY OCTOBER 3rd

We have a game today against a team from the 2nd division. It's our first game since Guinea so it will be a good chance to play the team I have in mind for the

Madagascar game, save for one or two slight injuries. It's hardly a great work out in the process as we labour to a 2-1 win. The one real bonus was Fikru, who having only arrived the night, before displayed great enthusiasm and no little ability. Given his status within the squad as the one they all clearly look up to, it's great that he seems to have such high regard for me too. If I can keep him happy, it might go a long way to success in the job.

MONDAY OCTOBER 4TH
The players have a day off today and finally there's more of warmth between Nadia and I. In fact she's positively delightful today, as she excitedly recounts more of the people she's been speaking to, including the eminent academic Ephraim Isaac. I don't actually know of him, but when she tells me he's offered her a position at Princeton University in New York, I'm genuinely pleased and obviously very proud of her. Where it leaves us, is for another time to discuss, but in terms of her career, it's almost perfect. An Ivy League university and in New York too, you couldn't have hand picked a better opportunity. We seem to bask in the glow of the news for the rest of the day.

TUESDAY OCTOBER 5TH
Here in Addis the rainy season looks to have finally left, to be replaced by sunshine! Even Atnafu, who despite the improvement in our relationship is still a "glass half empty" kind of guy, fails to knock me off my stride as the team continue to bond and develop.

I return back to the room to find Nadia musing over another job offer, from the Sheik this time. It's clearly sown seeds of doubt in her. A worrying development I conclude, clearly calling into question our future. Like nitro glycerine, this needs to be handled with care!

WEDNESDAY OCTOBER 6TH
It's the day before we leave for Madagascar and after training, I take my time going back, preferring to spend time with the guys and taking the easy way out rather than any possible conflicts back at the hotel. When I do return, Nadia's having dinner somewhere in the hotel, so I can pack and get ready for what will be a near week-long trip. When she arrives back later I'm already in bed

as we've an early 3am flight. We talk briefly before I'm waking up and heading off, Madagascar-bound!

THURSDAY OCTOBER 7TH

A brief stop off at the player's hotel reveals that they're not ready, so I head to the airport with Wandy and his wife, who's over from New York. I know we're playing with fire as we've instructions to be at the airport early to check in, but there's no sign of the players or staff yet.

Finally they arrive just in time for an anxious-looking Kenyan Airline staff who are clearly working on "super European" time to our "laid-back Ethiopian" time. Frankly, when it comes to flights and check ins, I'm with them, but this turns out to be the least of our troubles. It would appear that despite the Federation having checked and retained all the players' passports for the last three weeks; two have expired, one by 10 months!

I sit there in despair; it's only my first choice full backs, as well. Dr Elias and the rest try talking to airport officials to sort it out whilst I sit and silently weep. They even contact the general secretary of the Federation whose sage advice is to suggest that we have a "quiet" word with the officials, nudge nudge! Amazingly, after an hour of heated and desperate debate, we manage to get them on board and in the air.

We land at Nairobi to face the same headache, but at least we've time on our hands. Our connecting flight is three hours late on top of the three we were already expecting. Great start eh? Once again we negotiate our two fugitive escapees into another foreign territory and make the three hour trip to Madagascar. On arrival, we face another two hours at passport control courtesy of Bonnie and friggin Clyde! Finally, we're on the hour long minibus journey to our hotel where we arrive to no running water and a clearly mad and tanked up hotel owner!

FRIDAY OCTOBER 8TH

Understandably, we let the players lie in this morning in their new and communication-free surroundings. Yes, no internet, no phone, and our designated training pitch is, for now, unavailable to us. I alter training accordingly and wonder how long I can keep this fractious touring party happy. Meanwhile, the

Prince of Darkness, Atnafu is naturally suggesting - after the event of course - that we should have trained in the morning, despite the fact that our game will be in the afternoon. Although relations between us have softened, his "glass half empty" vision of life remains grating. I swallow hard and tell him that the field was booked for the morning but we couldn't use it then, REMEM-BER?? The players, as is their want, adapt well enough and training complete, we return to our hotel.

The players are a resilient bunch and get on with the things, but our six-man staff, seem to have a difference of opinion on everything. I wouldn't know for sure, as it's largely conducted in Ahmaric, adding to my feeling of isolation, but it's present all right. The end of the trip can't come soon enough already.

SATURDAY OCTOBER 9TH

It's the day before the game and we go into town to sort out alternative hotels closer to the stadium. Yes, we've all had enough of this one. Our hosts in all this have been marvellously co-operative and take us around some hotels, none of which we can agree on. Having kept my counsel throughout to silently witness all the fiasco, I pull rank here, save us waste any more time visiting hotels. I demand and receive a decision on which we all broadly agree (later Atnafu decides that the first hotel was better!).

Later that afternoon, we finally train on the pitch where the game will be held and I'm genuinely shocked and speechless. The setting was impressive enough, housed in a modern impressive-looking stadium in contrast to the old rickety stadium back in Addis, but the actual pitch is something to behold. The local media had mentioned it in passing and my hopes weren't exactly high, but even so, this beggared belief. It was basically a patchwork quilt of different coloured "grass", on top of well, dust. And it was rutted, and unmarked. When I recovered my composure, I decided we would revert to Plan B - to play the "English way". We will get the ball forward early and often to our big strikers and let them get on with it. I also named the team there and then. I was going to consult Atnafu that morning, but his constant negativity had got to me, so I effectively told him and Kitow, the goalkeeping coach, together.

I was intending to speak to the players collectively that night, but as the latest staff row broke out over the allocation of money, I decided it wasn't the right time and spoke in small groups instead. In hindsight, it was probably better that way anyway. I felt far more relaxed than I had all week.

SUNDAY OCTOBER 10TH

After the pre-game briefing, I find a church and experience my first mass conducted in French. Back to the hotel, I shave but decline to eat with the players for lunch, staying in my room instead. Truth is I've had a heavy cold all week and I'm off my food a bit. Also it saves watching the inevitable complaints about all aspects of the food given to them.

When they return, I speak to them collectively about the job in hand and their responsibilities. Even though Atnafu translates, I get more of a feeling as I've got closer to the players, that they understand most if not all of what I say in English. Even more surprising, my passionate tone induces a surprising and warm, spontaneous applause.

As we travel to the ground I sense a keen determination amongst the players and am suitably relaxed throughout the warm up. However, the start of the game soon heralds a change of mood, as we start nervously and nearly concede twice. After what seems an age, we finally settle down and at half time, we have successfully weathered the storm. I urge more of the same in the second half, knowing it will only be one moment that could win or lose the game. That moment duly arrives as Fikru, who's been immense for us up front, latches on to a long ball, rounds the keeper and rolls it into an empty net. Cue pandemonium from all, except me who's rather stupidly found himself watching proceedings from the stand after a silly moment of finger-wagging at the referee's assistant was reported to the referee. Humourless assistant he may be and it would barely be mentioned in any referee's report back in England, but it was stupid on my part and now I'm in purgatory for the rest of the game, as I try to relay instructions from far away. Eventually the whistle goes and though there's joy and happiness in the dressing room, my overwhelming feeling is one of relief. I'm emotionally and physically drained and I need my bed.

CHAPTER SIX

Familiar faces

MONDAY OCTOBER 11TH

I wake up and all I want to do is catch a flight back, but no, the nightmare must continue. Flights in and out of the island are few, but do we really have to wait until Wednesday before we're back? Oh right, we do it seems. So, cue another day fighting over the one working computer at the hotel, listening to people moan throughout the day, with no money effectively to buy phone cards. Never again, I tell myself, yeah right, until the next time! The only bright moments are those with the players bonding over Facebook or cameras which they're all taking pictures with and jostling to get in to shot with me. I can say I've really bonded with these guys over the last few days and feel like a big brother to them. They, and their efforts, have made everything else bearable…just!

TUESDAY OCTOBER 12TH

Finally our epic journey home is beginning. This whole week has had a Homer-esque feel about it and it's only now that I can reflect on the significance of our victory. I've got to come back and see how things are with me and Nadia, but this has bought a little time in Addis for me as Coach. Who knows what the repercussion of a loss would have been? As I contemplate all this on our return to Nairobi, from Madagascar, I suddenly realise that Atnafu isn't with us. I'm then told he's flown directly to Cairo for the FIFA conference. I had directly asked him about it the day before, yet he claimed not to be aware of it.

Of more pressing concern is another leg of the journey, namely a night in Nairobi. Suffice to say the journey's long and delayed, as we finally check into the hotel at 8pm, eat dinner, then bed for a 4.30am start the next morning. This has officially been the itinerary from Hades!

WEDNESDAY OCTOBER 13TH

We wake, groggy-eyed with Addis finally our destination. No further dramas mean we land at 10am. I've never been more delighted to be here. Now, the Federation have been conspicuous by their silence, save for one message of congratulations from the president, so it's genuinely a shock to see a welcoming committee including the president, greeting us at the airport. We're hugged, fussed over and taken to a hotel to enjoy breakfast before finally being allowed to retire. For me, it's back to the bosom of the Sheraton. Things seem fine with Nadia and we speak briefly and catch up before I hit the sack!

THURSDAY OCTOBER 14TH

Just when I thought I could plan my extended rest, I find out there are games to attend today (the Addis City Cup) and a meal given in honour of the players' achievements. With my thoughts already turning towards Nigeria in March, I begin to imagine how everyone would react if we got a result, or God help us, a victory? First things first though, and after I've taken in the game, it's off to the dinner. Most of the players are present and it's great that they've finally got some financial reward for their efforts. Equally unexpected, but no less pleasant was Yours Truly picking up some money too. I make a short speech thanking the players for their efforts and we all eat and go our separate ways.

FRIDAY OCTOBER 15TH

So, now it's time to pick up the threads with Nadia and see how things are. Unfortunately, I still feel like crap after the trip and it's all I can manage to go down to the pool area with her. It's definitely severe Man-flu I'm struggling with, but nonetheless I've no appetite and I'm not sure the sun sounds as appealing as staying in bed. But I grin and bear it for the sake of harmony.

SATURDAY OCTOBER 16TH

I think I may have under-played my flu, my head still feels like its exploding. True Man Flu! When I do leave the room for a mid-day radio interview, my interviewer fails to show. Back to bed!

SUNDAY OCTOBER 17TH

I wake up and go to church, come back and go down to the pool with Nadia. Things seem cordial, but I've another game to go to later, so it's not even possible to spend all day together and see what comes of it. This is underlined when the game drags on and Dr Elias insists on staying to the end. By the time I return, it's 7pm and dark.

MONDAY OCTOBER 18TH

Nadia confirms that she's leaving on Wednesday and that's probably the best thing all round. It's not been a happy time for either of us and I'm still laid low with whatever it was I caught in Madagascar. To be honest, I'm content to stay in bed most of the day, while she goes to the swimming pool area.

TUESDAY OCTOBER 19TH

The day that Atnafu finally made contact!! The last time I saw him, or didn't as the case turned out, was at the airport, when he did his Scarlett Pimpernel act. So, when he calls, I'm keen to work out his mood. He seems a little sheepish and makes no mention of Cairo, saying, "When should we meet?" Well, I'm not in a great mood to meet him, but mention that I'm at the Federation tomorrow afternoon, if he wants to see me then.

WEDNESDAY OCTOBER 20TH

Nadia is preparing to leave and having spent an enjoyable evening together last night, she's talked about coming back in a few weeks. If we can sort out a way forward, it would be good to have her here with me. Suddenly all seems rosy again, but I'm still wary. We'll need to do a lot of talking back in England when we meet, so we come back to Addis on a different page to when we arrived this time.

I go to the Federation to pick up our bonuses and Atnafu is there. I can tell he wants to talk about something, but I'm not letting him have it that easily whilst awaiting an explanation about Cairo that true to form never arrives. Instead, he pursues me even into the car as I try to head to the bank. I mentioned a while ago about bringing him some coaching materials from England and it seems that it's now that he wants to ask me about it again. Well, he's got some front I'll give him that. It may not have been down to him who went to Cairo, but he should have been honest with me when I asked him, I tell him directly, but without rancour.

Any small feeling of triumph at having handled that reasonably well soon fades as I go to the travel agency to change my ticket and the woman there says I could have changed it straightaway last time for free and now it will cost $100. Now, I know I did ask last time, and $100 right now, is precious. I keep it together and pay up, but it's another test of stoicism.

Nadia and I share a meal before heading to the airport and it's somehow fitting and indicative of the last four weeks, that at the airport we go in different doors and through the nightmare of bureaucracy that is Addis airport, we miss each other and don't even get to say goodbye.

THURSDAY OCTOBER 21ST

Now, I must confess, there's never a dull moment when Nadia's around and today with her gone, it's nothing but dull. I've still no appetite and surviving on a diet of Pepsi and milkshakes, but even a now-annoyingly-persistent-illness, can't detract from the boredom. When I tune in later to watch Liverpool v Napoli, in the Europa League, I witness arguably the dullest game that I've seen for a long, long time. But somehow, I'm not surprised either. I've run out of books to read too, so the weekend and return home, can't come soon enough.

FRIDAY OCTOBER 22ND

Wandy rings early and we meet up to go jeans shopping. It's become a nightmare in England looking for fashionable jeans to fit these days. Despite my current ailments, I think room service at the hotel is beginning to take its toll, so I may as well go cheap over here. £16 for a pair of comfort fit Levi jeans with Iceberg buttons and Wrangler patch later, and I'm sorted and well on the road to middle age!

SATURDAY OCTOBER 23RD

Finally, Sir David Richards and agent Dave arrive from England. The way things have been going here, I'm desperate for some familiar and friendly faces. I know the moment they both leave it will be like they've never visited, but I'll worry about that another time. For now it's good that they're here, and I can bask in Sir David's influence, in particular.

So, off we go to the Presidential palace (President, very impressive man, with a fine memory for a man in his 80's) and later in the evening there's an impressive dinner banquet, where Sir David is regaled and I sit comfortably and enjoy an evening, for the first time in weeks.

SUNDAY OCTOBER 24TH

More of the same as it's an early morning visit to the new academy on the outskirts of Addis. It's still very much under construction but actually quite impressive, or at least will be when it's finished. Soon though, it's time for them to depart, and as we see them off at the airport, I'm comforted by the fact that I'm not far behind.

MONDAY OCTOBER 25TH

It's my third time back in England, so I'm feeling a little guilty now even though there's basically nothing to do and this is a genuine pre-booked holiday time to celebrate my younger brother's wedding in Canada, no less. It's early evening when I eventually arrive back and it won't be long until I'm back at the airport with daughter number two, jetting off to Canada.

TUESDAY OCTOBER 26TH

Everything seems straightforward, flights are booked, Mark's going to the airport too, so we're all sorted and raring to go.

WEDNESDAY OCTOBER 27TH

It's an early start as our flight is at 8am from Heathrow, so it's something of a challenge to get both daughter two and Nadia out of the house in time. I just about manage it though, and we head off to meet Mark in Windsor to park the car and then catch a taxi to the airport.

Before long we're off to Toronto and whoa what a welcome from Canadian immigration, as they basically crawled all over us like a cheap suit! It was a full two hours before we finally left the airport bound for our motel (I insisted on booking at LEAST one night's accommodation in advance!).

When we arrive, eventually, with the help of a hire car, the girls are shattered, so I go to see my brother and his bride to be, at her parents' house. They had generously offered to put us up, but there's already a houseful of Onuoras with my older brother's family and I didn't want to impose anymore. They're lovely warm people and it's nice for us all to put faces to names after all this time. Still, we go back to the motel and at last it's sleep time.

THURSDAY OCTOBER 28TH

An early start today as there's an arranged trip to Niagara Falls by minibus. We make it to Niagara via a trip to a Winery and it's probably the best day, all in all, that I've had in several weeks. It's good to see family members meeting, laughing and enjoying the stunning sights.

However, we still haven't booked a hotel for that night as we decided to book the rest of our accommodation when we arrived. The family house is in Burlington, about 20km from Toronto. So, as some of the party prepare to go into Toronto for the night, we're still not booked in. Eventually we head to Toronto to stay the night there.

FRIDAY OCTOBER 29TH

It's the day before the wedding and with a generously sized hire car, I'm the delivery man on supplies of food and wine for that evening's rehearsal dinner. After last night's shenanigans, I've taken charge of hotel duties, booking us a two-night stay in a hotel close to the church and reception.

The rehearsal dinner is great too; lots more relatives and familiar faces arrive and we're clad in traditional Nigerian dress, eating traditional foods.

Everyone seems to be having a great time and it's not until gone midnight before we head back.

SATURDAY OCTOBER 30TH

The day of the wedding. It's a beautiful clear day in picture postcard, Burlington. The day is special, made doubly so by all the people who've travelled from far and wide, including relatives from the States that I've not seen for years. The service is well conducted and the reception takes place at a venue that backs on to the lake behind. If you looked up the definition of the word idyllic, you would probably see a picture of the venue right there. By the end of the evening, as we're typically the last to make it home, it's difficult to know how it could have been improved upon.

SUNDAY OCTOBER 31ST

The morning after the night before and fatigue's set in. We have a vague plan to return our hire car in good time, buy a few presents, before leaving on the late flight. We do make a token gesture of going to the shopping mall, but the truth is, that our hearts aren't in it and we manage a little food there but little else.

We spend some more chill time with Sarah's parents and say our goodbyes before heading off at last to the airport. Nadia's travelling on from there to New York to stay at Princeton and see the place where she's been offered a job, so she won't be travelling back with us.

MONDAY NOVEMBER 1ST

Mark's car breaks down so we take a taxi. I then pick up my car and we're heading back to Bristol. I drop off my daughter and try to plan the next few days carefully before I head back to Addis. I've an interview to do, possibly on Thursday, with Alan Green for BBC World Service. So, I'll need to spin things out until then, at least.

TUESDAY NOVEMBER 2ND

Any guilt I had about being away from work is offset by the fact that my salary has still NOT been paid! In fact, I go down to Exeter to see my eldest daughter at university there and end up having to borrow £10 for petrol to get me home!

When later that night my son leaves me his bankcard for the next day, I reflect that borrowing money off your student kids is not quite how I imagined things should be. In fact, I would have to say that it's somewhat less than my finest parenting moment.

WEDNESDAY NOVEMBER 3RD

Still no sign of any salary, so I spend my time putting together that IKEA furniture that's been sitting in my bedroom waiting to be put together by magic! I'm not big on DIY, but suddenly I've got the bug and spend my time going back to IKEA, window shopping ready for tomorrow when, I'm told, the money will be in my account.

THURSDAY NOVEMBER 4TH

How does the song go? "If tomorrow never comes?" Well, tomorrow has now arrived and there's STILL no money. It looks like I'm here until the start of the weekend at least and now, in respect of my job, I NEED to get back. I know how things work, I'll be the one criticised and no-one will back me up. That's how it will pan out. I do the BBC interview with Alan Green. I've never met him or spoken to him before, but he's very professional with me and genuinely keen to find out all about life in Ethiopia. Meanwhile, more contact with David revealed that my salary was now promised once again for, tomorrow! Yeah right, I'll believe it when I see it now!

FRIDAY NOVEMBER 5TH

Bonfire Night, and apart from waiting and checking my bank account, I've nothing planned. There's a glimmer of light insofar as a cheque I paid in HAS cleared, so now I can at least, eat and drink. I celebrate by going to see the team at Tomorrow's People. I enjoyed my time there and it's good to see them all. Besides if things continue as they are, I might need my old job back! I go for a few drinks with a few of them, before heading back home.

SATURDAY NOVEMBER 6TH

It's Saturday and still no real plan. I hang about, watch the football results (my old team Gillingham lose in the FA Cup to Dover), but it's not until later on, that I leave the flat. I've arranged for a drink with an ex of mine and it's genuinely nice to see her and catch up. It's perfectly cordial too when her current beau arrives too to join us, but nonetheless I make my excuses after a short time, and head off.

SUNDAY NOVEMBER 8TH

Get up early and go to church. Later on I exchange a couple of e mails with the president and like I expected, he's preparing the ground to save face for my non-arrival yet, and basically blame me. Now, I've come to understand how far I can push things, and with whom. With the president I've always been able to push things quite a bit, as I know he likes my passion for the job. So, I make it clear that I'm having none of it and he should look elsewhere for his scapegoat. Round One to me, it seems, but I doubt I'll escape lightly when it really comes down to it. Watch this space.

MONDAY NOVEMBER 9TH

Another day and it's the same old, same old. More phone calls, more promises, but still no money. I'm starting to fear again the possibilities of ever returning to my job. After all when it comes down to it, there's been no change here since I left. One result against a team ranked just above us does not suddenly make me an über-coach, on the wish list of club chairmen the world over.

So, I know I've got to return at the earliest possible opportunity and be ready for when that arises. In the meantime, well, I can still make a mean lasagne! Thankfully, my culinary effort means that my son bless him, doesn't have to scramble around for food at the end of a long day.

TUESDAY NOVEMBER 10TH

See above, right down to making another lasagne, it truly is Groundhog Day now! Judge Judy, 60 Minute Makeover etc, I feel like I'm either unemployed or a student…again!

WEDNESDAY NOVEMBER 11TH

Sweet joy, a ray of light that becomes a huge unmistakeable shaft! The money is in, or at least part of it, so I attempt to make up for lost time by embarking on the mother of all spending sprees. I even manage to book a flight ticket back that night, all of which leaves me almost back in the same position by lunchtime. But no matter, the rest will be in my account by the end of the day, so there won't be any further problems…will there??

After a dash to Temple Meads train station, I disembark at Reading to take the Heathrow Express and a quick check in. I'm once again Addis-bound, to see what's in store.

THURSDAY NOVEMBER 12TH

I touchdown early and though it's great to see Wandy again, I'm quickly filled by foreboding as he tells me about how people have all been asking where I've been. I roll my eyes silently, here we go again. I'll be hung out to dry again, no doubt. I resolve not to care right now and after a short sleep, I head to the Federation.

I'm greeted warmly, as ever, by the lovely people who work there. However, I soon learn there have been one or two subtle changes. John, the technical director, has finally been assigned to work closer with me, which we'd both been pushing for, and the new man assigned to the team Mr Afework, is a warm, avuncular guy, who I already get on well with.

So, what brought on this change, I wonder? Well, I know that FIFA gave them a blasting in a recent report, but even so, for me this is a welcome change. After all, John and I have even got a desk in the office from where we can work on a daily basis!

CHAPTER SEVEN

Close but no cigar

FRIDAY NOVEMBER 13TH

Went to my desk at the Federation and with the help of John and Atnafu, we picked a squad to train ahead of the forthcoming CECAFA tournament in Tanzania. Once again, it's hardly ideal, effectively picking your team and subs three weeks ahead. But this is how it's done. I'm definitely short on details on some players, so I rely on John's input whilst resolving to keep the core of the squad that went to Madagascar. We arrange letters to be sent to the clubs asking to release players to begin training next week. I learn later that this letter was never sent!

SATURDAY NOVEMBER 14TH

I'm still on GMT which means I'm going to bed late here. However, no problems today as I can sleep in at last. I was up late doing my blog for Four Four Two magazine in England, so it's only at 2pm that I wake up, ready for the two games at the Abebe Bikila Stadium this afternoon. The first one is predictably a snore-fest, but the second is of a higher tempo and far more exciting. I get back in time to catch a little of the results from England including Man Utd drawing 2-2 with Aston Villa and Liverpool losing to Stoke in the early evening kick off. I'm always looking to learn from managers in their game plans and also, their post-match interviews. Sir Alex doesn't even mention his own team. He lavishes praise on Aston Villa's young side. In contrast, I recognise in Roy Hodgson's downbeat demeanour, the different challenge of managing such a big club as Liverpool especially with all the ownership issues they've had.

SUNDAY NOVEMBER 15TH

Very early start today as we are travelling to Yirgalem, in the south of the county, to watch a game. We pick up Bertokan, a young, pretty journalist who wants to attend the game to do a radio report. I do love travelling on long journeys here, watching the city give way to the countryside, with people hard at work to eke out a living to feed themselves and their families. It has some stunning scenery with vast terrain and rolling hills. You can just drift off, deep in thought.

The game is a fractious local derby that ends up in a 2-2 draw. After a little searching, we finally locate a typically packed bar, to watch Arsenal edge out Everton 2-1. The Blues have made a typical slow start to the season, but David Moyes is a great manager, so I know we'll be fine. The moment the game ends, the rest of the bar empties and a cheer goes up. It seems to be an almost 50-50 split between Man Utd fans and Arsenal fans, as I understand it, a situation underscored by the fact that from sitting squashed at the back, we now instantly have front row seats for Chelsea v Sunderland. A good day for Arsenal is made even better as Sunderland overwhelm the champions 3-0. Wandy's gutted and I confess to teasing him mercilessly. He decides to retire to bed early citing "tiredness" from the drive. Hmmm, not sure about that, Wandy normally loves a beer!

MONDAY NOVEMBER 16TH

An early start and we appear to have picked up another passenger on our return to Addis. Marcos, the hotel owner where we stayed last night, is visiting a sick friend in Addis and comes along for a ride. Bless poor Bertokan. She sits in the back with him and in four hours, he barely pauses for breath! I feel for her, but manage to drift off in my thoughts again. I do like her though; she's very professional in her approach to reporting and also has a good knowledge of the players too. I'll definitely be keeping her on my side, perhaps as an unofficial press PA. Melaku is meant to do the job for the Federation, but is always assigned to other duties, so Bertokan could be very useful in that role.

Back at the Federation, it becomes clear that my plans for a training week, from tomorrow, have been pretty much shredded. First of all, the secretary at the Federation didn't send off those letters as I asked. In truth there may have been some confusion last week because the priority was to send the names back to the tournament organisers, but still it has a knock on effect.

TUESDAY NOVEMBER 17TH

I decide not to even try to intervene in what appears to be a classic case of club v country. Atnafu is working himself up about it, so I let him chase up all the loose ends while I take one of those chill pills I've been popping lately. Mentally, I tell myself a week's preparation will be fine.

WEDNESDAY NOVEMBER 18TH

Although I'm proud of my desk at the Federation, sadly, I don't have a key for the office. So, it's a case of taking a guess at when it might be open!

In the best tradition of life in an office, I try to look extremely busy doing nothing. I've often offered to help with the delivery of coaching courses here or even helping Melaku the press officer, as he seems permanently stressed. However, my offers have never been taken up, so I've given up asking and content myself to write up some coaching sessions.

Unconfirmed reports are that we're leaving in a week's time, so once again it's fingers crossed that there's no injuries between now and then, as players cannot be replaced.

THURSDAY NOVEMBER 19TH

Less than a week to go and the players still don't appear to have kit, boots or up to date passports. Still, I'm the very picture of stoicism and I'm looking forward to the tournament and all the other incidentals that always seem to eventually work themselves out. Que sera sera.

FRIDAY NOVEMBER 20TH

It's been like Groundhog Day this week: a few hours at the Federation followed by one or two attempts to get to grips with my distance learning Law course. However, there is no confirmation of what day we're actually flying or when the squad will assemble. It's essentially a waiting game whilst being fully prepared to go at a moment's notice.

SATURDAY NOVEMBER 21ST

No Premier League games today and I've decided to give the studies a break. The president is back now and wastes little time in laying down a marker about John NOT going with us to Tanzania. Events have advanced since then anyway as John's had enough and tendered his resignation as Technical Director. The president tells me he was rude to him and John tells me that he was not allowed to do his job properly. Despite my plea for him to reconsider, John has given in his notice. I'm not sure where that leaves things now, I hadn't seen or spoken to John much recently and I didn't realise the extent of his frustrations. But it's definitely not a good development, as I see it.

SUNDAY NOVEMBER 22ND

Off on our travels again today, this time to Adama to watch the home side play Sebeta. It's nice to get out of Addis and having stayed in Adama back in July when I first arrived, I'm happy to return. The locals give me a warm welcome. The game's okay too, and it's nice to see a few other players who I can keep an eye on for the future. We soon head back because we need to prepare for the arrival of the players tomorrow.

MONDAY NOVEMBER 23RD

We arrive early at the stadium to be greeted by NO players! It transpires that the games have NOT been cancelled and as a result, the players have stayed with their clubs for the games tomorrow night. It's a little embarrassing, not least because the BBC have come over to do a piece on the Great Ethiopian Run this weekend and a piece on me for Football Focus. So, instead, we go to where St George train and get some improvised shots there. It was interesting to watch them train, they're the biggest club in Ethiopia and supply many of the players for the national team. Strangely, they continue to struggle in the league under their Italian coach. He's a nice guy though and very accommodating.

TUESDAY NOVEMBER 24TH

I've now adjusted to the fact that I won't have the players, so it's just a watching brief tonight. Most of the national players are on show, so I'll be anxiously watching to make sure they come through unscathed.

WEDNESDAY NOVEMBER 25TH

It's officially the first day when I have the players. We have a little warm down on the pitch, at the stadium, but not before I attend a press conference that starts out fractious and ends in grudging respect. I must be a glutton for this, as it was my idea. However, by the end, I come through, I think, with some new level of respect from the journos…..until next time!

Any good feeling soon evaporates, as I'm told in a phone call that we're to leave TONIGHT for Tanzania. Tonight? When I've been asking all week? This has to be some sort of joke. Unfortunately it's not. One heated phone conversation with the president later and I'm in his office having a frank exchange of views! Eventually a measure of common sense ensues and the flight is put back 48 hours. Really, we haven't got boots for the players or had our jabs. What's more, not all of the visas have been sorted. I think the president is a good guy, but he doesn't always appreciate those rather crucial items.

THURSDAY NOVEMBER 26TH

We'll be flying out overnight on Friday, to Tanzania. Not ideal to take an overnight flight, but it's better than the alternative and at least I can have another day's training in Addis. At least the players look bright and sharp again, they seemed to have settled into their pre-Madagascar groove. The new guys don't look out of place either.

FRIDAY NOVEMBER 27TH

Our final training session before departure and the usual problem of money to buy boots re-surfaces. The players have spoken of it for the last few days and I've pressed the case. However, there is still no sign and it's frustrating how everything is constantly hovering on the brink and left to the last minute. Thankfully the money does come…or most of it, meaning that even though its 3pm in the afternoon and we're flying that evening, some players still need to go out and buy boots. Cue a mad dash to pick up some more money and skip around the city in pursuit of boots. As we leave the airport and surprisingly without further drama, the best I could dare contemplate was progress out of our Group of Death, to the latter stages.

SATURDAY NOVEMBER 28TH

It was very hot and humid when we arrived in Dar Es Salaam, in the small hours of the morning. We are picked up by our driver for the tournament, Ismael, a wizened but warm guy. Our co-ordinator Wilfred, is an ex player, who is still quite young. Bed was the order of the day and I cancelled breakfast for the guys, insisting that they sleep, before getting up for lunch at 1pm. Atnafu immediately suggested that maybe they should have breakfast. Oh please no, not another Madagascar trip! I repeated my assertion sternly and resolved not to let things go as far as they did previously. No chance. Not this time!

We slept and in the afternoon attended a vibrant and colourful opening ceremony complete with dancers, singers, acrobats and the usual pyrotechnics. It's a 12 team tournament comprising three groups of four teams. We're in a tough looking group with Uganda, Kenya and Malawi. The hosts kicked off the tournament losing to one of the three invited teams, a strong-looking Zambian outfit. I enjoyed it all, especially inside the magnificent and modern national stadium. However, what disappointed me were the rows and rows of empty seats. It wasn't even half full and this inside a stadium designed to hold 60,000. Still, we were finally under way and I was determined to do well and enjoy the experience.

SUNDAY NOVEMBER 29TH

Our first training session was scheduled for 11am. It gave me enough time to go to church, courtesy of the ever-reliable, Ismael. In the time I've spent in the job, I've been to church in Ethiopia (Ahmaric), Madagascar (French) and now Tanzania (Swahili). It was a different experience again and I enjoyed it before my mind raced off thinking about tomorrow's game.

Later that afternoon, after training, the staff went to the local shopping mall and mindful of the stifling heat, we picked up energy drinks, bananas and chocolate for the players and an ever-needy bottle of red wine and a bag of sweets, for the coach! True to form Atnafu questioned the energy drinks and whilst I too would have preferred isotonic ones, to the red bull type, it further irritated me. Why oh why, can't he just keep quiet?

MONDAY NOVEMBER 30TH

All four teams from the group stayed in the same hotel and mingled happily. I sought out Bobby Williamson, the Ugandan coach, who would be our first opponents. They were defending champions and as their national coach, he had a great record. I thought it would be good to pick his brains and share experiences this week.

We travelled by police escort to the ground due in no small part to the traffic in Dar Es Salaam. It just never seemed to move…...ever! Goodness knows how people get on with their lives here, but as in most African cities I've visited; it seemed to have a spirit and a vibrancy, to compensate.

For the game itself, the stadium was still disappointingly empty, but as the temperature nudged the mid-30s, it was clear that this would be a big factor in the game too. And so it proved. We made a strong start, surprising the well organised Ugandans with our passing and movement. When, after half an hour, we made it 1-0, thanks to a goal from Shimeles Bekele, things looked good. Sadly, it wasn't to last. We conceded a soft penalty to go in level at the break. When I walked in to the dressing rooms after a couple of minutes of the interval (I usually have a period of reflection alone first), I saw the players slumped on the floor, exhausted by the heat. I rallied them as best I could, but right there and then, I'd have taken a creditable draw. Unfortunately, our goalkeeper allowed a harmless looking cross to drop nicely to one of the Ugandans who duly converted. Despite a late and brave rally, that was that, we'd lost our first game. I told the players not to be too despondent as we'd given a good account of ourselves and we would remain positive for the Kenyan game in two days' time.

Later, as I took time to reflect on the game, I found myself getting more and more frustrated. I was obviously disappointed that a mistake that cost us the game. However, it was more than that. Not for the first time, the players had been late on to the bus. Also, Kitow, the goalkeeping coach, had forgotten the cones for the warm up and had to borrow some off Uganda. Then, we had Atnafu's contribution to the day, which I would suggest, was non-existent. I resolved to reserve my words of wisdom until tomorrow. But let's just say, inside, I was a little miffed.

TUESDAY DECEMBER 1ST

We had a light training session this morning and headed off to the beach nearby, principally to use the water to shake off any heavy legs from the day before. What I didn't anticipate was that these guys, unused to seeing the sea, came alive like excitable 10-year olds. In short, it was just the tonic needed and I bought ice creams all round to further the bonhomie. When Atnafu questioned whether the ice creams were a suitable dietary aid, I'd had enough. Later that evening, I spoke to him in his room about his small-mindedness and his decision to question EVERYTHING I said. I reminded him of his real job out here which was to assist in all matters, something which he'd improved on since those early days in July (I made sure I told him that too, so it wasn't all critical), but still needed much attention. My Atnafu-work is a continual work in progress and will not be completed anytime soon, methinks.

The defeat the previous day to Uganda now forgotten, we find a beach to unwind and escape the heat of Dar Es Salaam. It does the trick, two days later we defeat our old enemy, the Kenyans!

WEDNESDAY DECEMBER 2ND

The logistics of trying to accommodate 12 teams training on the same pitch are now beginning to look strained. We are each given an hour slot, but it becomes clear that some have preferable times to others. It's difficult, although the coaches are all understanding other than the Zambian's Italian coach, who along with his two countrymen, who comprised their staff, seemed to have a touch of arrogance about them.

Similarly, the timing of our meals back at the hotel, was beginning to grate. It can't be easy feeding four teams out of one kitchen, at the times specifically requested by each of the four coaches. I'm also sure that their indifference, at times, didn't help matters. Finally, despite my frustration, I have to remember that hotel staff, anywhere in the world, are not paid enough to share the same concerns as the guests.

Returning to my room at the end of the day, I resolved to roll with the punches as best I could without getting too stressed, just at the same time the power went out, leaving me in darkness and with no TV. I reached for the red wine, an inspired purchase!

THURSDAY DECEMBER 3RD

Our next game is against Kenya and from the start we look sluggish. The effects of the game two days ago are still there to see and it doesn't augur well. So, when we get a free kick on the edge of the box and Shimeles finds the top corner, Ronaldo-style, it's a welcome relief. And the little man hasn't finished yet. He collects a slide-rule pass from the equally impressive Omod, to make it 2-0 just before half time. I remind them of being disciplined and to carry on playing the same way in the second half. By and large they do, until I make what in hindsight was a mistake, taking off skipper Samson with 10 minutes to go. They'd been galvanised by an open goal miss from our right winger Jonathan which would have put us out of sight. Then having piled on the pressure, they pull a goal back. They, of course, go in search of the equaliser, but mercifully we hold out. We have our first win under our belts.

It was an enjoyable evening, with the beer tasting as good as it had since we'd arrived. We were comfortable winners despite the late rally from Kenya.

Doing the maths, we realised that a draw in our final group game should be enough to see us progress to the quarter finals.

FRIDAY DECEMBER 4TH

With just one day between games, I had to manage the guys effectively. We had a very light session with another trip to the beach. Tomorrow's game would again be at the hottest part of the day and it was a game from which we would need something. Word had reached us, from back in Addis, that the win against our old rivals, Kenya had pleased everyone. Unfortunately, for me personally, as the coach, yesterday's elation had given way to today's concern. We really need to progress out of our group to keep my "project" on track.

SATURDAY DECEMBER 5TH

Our final group game against Malawi and the players are in good spirits. They appear as ready as they ever will be and that gives me a warm feeling. Malawi already had four points from their two games and as another of the invited teams, was considered strong opposition. And so it proved once again in the searing heat. They looked strong, first to every ball. They dominated proceedings early on and after 20 minutes, duly went ahead with an excellent free kick. It was no more than they deserved. They continued in a similar vein for the rest of the half and I was silently hoping that we could get in at half time only a goal down. Then, out of nowhere, Omod stepped forward. Picking a ball up from deep, he drove forward, pulled the trigger and thanks to a slight deflection, found the net. Their keeper had no chance. At the interval, I took the edge off what was going to be, before the equaliser, a fairly stern rebuke. Somehow, I had to rouse them from their slumber. However, the goal had done just that and I made a few tactical points and urged caution as the result at the moment kept their hopes alive. The second half was far more even and we were good value for the eventual 1-1 draw. We now had to wait on other results.

The next game played, after ours, involved Burundi, who were in another group, but on the same points as us, but with a better goal difference. However, a 2-0 loss to Rwanda evened out the goal difference and with our goals scored now coming into the equation, we would now qualify without having to wait for the other result in our group. I was relieved and felt emotionally drained. To get to the quarter finals was a significant achievement. What's more, our style of play had won us many new admirers amongst the neutrals, and a few native Tanzanians.

Sadly, it was out of keeping with the day when later in the evening, sharing a beer outside, a row developed amongst the staff about the kit to be worn for the next game. Of all the things to fall out about!! I'm not sure why I became involved, but against all instincts, I did. It ended up with me shouting at the Team Leader, Mr Afework, before storming off to bed. It was a total overreaction and I knew it. I resolved to apologise the next morning. Even worse, I'd left half a pint of beer on the table, truly scandalous!

SUNDAY DECEMBER 6TH

I woke up and immediately sought out Mr Afework, to say sorry for the night before. He generously accepted and it was forgotten just as quickly. I like this guy even more, I thought.

The next game was not until Tuesday, so the players had a day off. They relax whilst we went to the mall again. Mr Afework and Dr Gemechu, had developed something of a double act based largely on the latter continually asking for money from the former, who had positioned himself, somewhat self reverentially and with more than a twinkle in his eye, as the patrician figure parsimoniously in charge of all the cash. I loved the knockabout spirit of it all, two grown men, older than me, playing the fool at every opportunity. It certainly made a change from Madagascar, the memory of my six days there, still causing me to shudder.

MONDAY DECEMBER 7TH

The day before the game and as luck would have it, we arrived to train as Zambia, our quarter final opponents, were in the middle of their session. Once again, I detected an arrogant air about the coach and little of the bonhomie that I experienced when we first bumped into each other. Sometimes you'll foster a sense of injustice or grievance for the galvanising effect it can have and here I found my own moment. I prepared the guys thoroughly, ironing out one or two weaknesses I'd detected against Malawi.

I also had another talk with Atnafu, despite me not wanting to. He's just hard to ignore. Even the lovely Dr Gemechu who has a ray of sunshine permanently about him, has noticed his negative aura. He'd still not stepped up and made any significant contribution to the trip and I particularly chided him for his introspection before games when the players' morale needed boosting just by a quiet word here and there. His usual modus operandi is to slump in a chair and give the impression of disinterest or even worse, being the nervous sort, giving off a lot of nervous energy. He gave me that deep look of his, which in films would possibly precede a sudden, violent attack. In his case, it was just a case of him contemplating his next response. I stuck to my guns and urged him to rouse himself before games and not leave it exclusively to me.

TUESDAY DECEMBER 8TH

The day of the game and the crowds had started to fill the stadium thanks to the organisers relaxing the ticket prices. If we were heavy underdogs against the tournament favourites, the reception as we entered the arena made it clear that we were definitely the neutrals' favourites.

Taking this as our inspiration, we dominated the early proceedings, going ahead through a header from a set play by our midfield colossus Tesfaye Alabachew. When Omod doubled the lead after half an hour and the Zambians were reduced to 10 men on the stroke of half time, the game was ours to lose. I tried to contain the enthusiasm at half time by telling the players that they could make the second half as easy or as difficult as they wanted depending on their approach. Of course they chose the latter!

Our other goalkeeper began the fun by letting a harmless looking cross that would have embarrassed an under 12 goalkeeper, sail over his head and into the net. Cue Bottle-rage from Yours Truly, as water bottles and stopwatches were launched skywards with all the force I could muster.

The next 10 minutes combined comedic defending at one end, with a glut of missed opportunities at the other. In short, these are ingredients designed to make any coach descend slowly but surely into madness! However, in a similar vein to the Kenyan game, we held out to record a famous victory. I was obviously overjoyed but not too surprised that none of the opposing bench offered so much as a handshake at the end, choosing instead, to walk straight down the tunnel.

I later heard that the Zambian head coach had laid all the blame for the result at the door of the referee for the sending off, this despite us being 2-0 up at the time!

And so it was a semi-final clash in three days with the mighty Cote D'Ivoire, who despite not having the stellar names based in Europe, were still a very strong side. I was mighty impressed when I watched them a couple of days ago against our group opponents, Malawi. They were a physically strong side and an imposing unit too. But, I was looking on the bright side and they would be great preparation for our clash with the Nigerians next March.

As we all basked in the glow of the result that night, my only worry was the form of Shimeles who'd gone off the boil since the opening games. Perhaps understandable, if it was solely due to tiredness, but he's normally a lively presence around the group. Today, he was anything but. I know for a fact that a number of agents had been ringing him up and my fear was that they'd turned his head. I took time to speak to both him and Omod about it, but Omod was less of a worry having kept his form consistently high. I would have to watch that situation carefully.

WEDNESDAY DECEMBER 9TH

Another chance for the players to rest today as we don't play until Friday. Once again, I headed to the mall for provisions. Our story was now the story of the tournament, as most if not all, had dismissed us, pre-tournament, as mere cannon fodder. To find ourselves contesting a semi-final was beyond the wildest expectations of everyone with the exception of the coach who had stars in his eyes! It was now time to dream about lifting the trophy itself. No-one day dreams quite like me, given half a chance!

THURSDAY DECEMBER 10TH

Our final, meaningful training session this morning and with only four teams left, we were afforded all the time and space we needed, in which to train. We covered all that was needed before heading back with a mandate to eat and drink plenty, with kick-off time scheduled, once again, for the middle of the afternoon.

FRIDAY DECEMBER 11TH

I felt a little flat going in to the game and I don't know why. I may have exhausted myself emotionally with Atnafu, but I'm not on full cylinders as per normal. Not sure it would ever be noticeable to anyone but myself as the clues aren't obvious, but I know for sure.

Despite a bright start to the game, it's clear to me that the power play of Cote D'Ivoire is making headway in a game where as well as Shimeles, one or two are beginning to look a little leggy. Hardly surprising given the heat and we do well to get to the interval level at 0-0. I urge one more effort, but when they take the lead with 15 minutes remaining, there's an inevitability about it. Despite a late brave rally, the dream is over. Still, I'm proud of them and tell them so. Now, we must try to get third place. I hope it's the hosts Tanzania, who despite their opening game defeat, have shown significant improvement. They duly defeat our old friends Uganda on penalties, so once again we'll play them, this time for a third place prize of $10,000.

Battle fatigued and weary, I tell the players to relax tomorrow. Another training session would be unnecessary. We will just turn up on the day; see who's fit, and play.

We've located an Ethiopian restaurant in the city, makes a change from the standard fare at the hotel, and the guys are happy again!

SATURDAY DECEMBER 12TH

Yesterday's disappointment gives way to pride. I'm delighted with our achieve-ments thus far and the new respect we've garnered in all quarters. However, we still have a little way to go. I told the players to meet at 11am for a walk and they're late again as they have been on several occasions this week. Their time-keeping was in marked contrast to the other teams staying in the hotel. I'm probably more annoyed because I let the players rest whilst I know Uganda played extra time, but still got up to train. More lessons to learn for the future.

The president has arrived and everyone's especially pleased to see him be-cause he'd brought more dollars for us, as we've run out of our original 10 days allowance. We also take in a local Ethiopian restaurant that night and as I see the happy faces, I feel vindicated by my decision.

SUNDAY DECEMBER 12TH

We leave for the stadium for the last time and I'm really up for the game. I even mistakenly get the players out earlier than intended due to that dodgy watch I asked Wandy to get the other day, now half an hour fast! I've also changed the system from my usual 4-3-3 to a 3-5-2 because of injuries and to accommo-date Samuel, the one player who hasn't started a game yet in the tournament.

The game itself is a wildly entertaining free for all, as both teams eschew even the basics of defending. We open the scoring before another calamitous goalkeeping error brings them level. We score again to go in to the break 2-1 up and thereafter, I persist with the system which I might have changed at half time. We then gift wrap another equaliser, courtesy of another goalkeep-ing error. I'm afraid to say that goalkeeping is the Achilles heel of Ethiopian football. They score a great goal to lead for the first time 3-2 and with 15 min-utes to go, we look doomed. Then we equalise again through the lion-hearted Alabachew, before gift wrapping their fourth and decisive goal. Any one of a number of factors from our preparation, the change of system and the lack of a goalkeeper, could be used as an excuse for the defeat. But the blunt truth is that Uganda have proved our nemesis again. It feels just as bad, possibly worse than losing to Cote D'Ivoire.

We hang around long enough to see Tanzania crowned champions, defeat-ing Cote D'Ivoire in the final, 1-0, thanks to a penalty. They gave out all the prize money and individual awards after the final and I cursed again. What I'd have given for the $10,000 and how we could have used it effectively for kit, boots etc.

MONDAY DECEMBER 13TH

I wake up and it suddenly feels like you've overstayed your welcome at a party. Everyone just wants to go home. A few phone calls later and, hey presto, we're on the earlier flight to Addis. We head for the airport and say our goodbyes to Wilfred and Ismael, who've looked after us royally for the last two weeks. No time for presents, so I get everyone to sign a football each for them.

On the flight back, I reflect on the lessons learnt and the mistakes made as well as all the positives. It's actually a magical journey back, as we have a great view of the imposing Mount Kilimanjaro, to accompany my thoughts of wonder and awe. I feel very blessed to be living and working in Africa. It's not without its challenges and difficulties, but it seems to have touched my soul in a way that I wouldn't have understood, had I not experienced it directly for myself. The last fortnight in Dar Es Salaam, has been an enriching part of that process.

Talking of magical, we get a warm reception back at the airport and it's clear the tournament has made stars out of Omod and Shimeles. That situation will no doubt pose its own tricky problems which I'll have to deal with over the next few days. It's also garnered some hard-won respect for me amongst the watching public and press. Job done I think, now get me back to England for Christmas - quickly.

It's nice to see Wandy too and we can't help but have a beer or two watching Man Utd v Arsenal. Wandy warns me there will be a real rivalry in the bars that screen the games, so when it all gets a bit fractious, after United take the lead, we get up and leave. I'm too contented to be dragged down by all that. Besides I'm tired.

The staff: from left to right, Kitow (gk coach), Mr Afework (team leader), Dr Getachew, Wilfred (driver), Jack (physio), Wilfred (team liaison), Yours Truly (resplendent in understated tracksuit !!)

CHAPTER EIGHT

I'm coming home for Christmas

TUESDAY DECEMBER 14TH

A lazy day catching up with messages from friends all offering congratulations on the result. It's nice really and even if a few, particularly in Addis, are jumping on a bandwagon they never previously looked like doing, in the end, I guess that's just human nature. Let it go, roll with it sunshine, let sleeping dogs lie!

WEDNESDAY DECEMBER 15TH

Not exactly rock 'n' roll, but I've missed two weeks of my law course that I'm already hopelessly behind in, so it's back to the grind as realistically there's very little chance of me doing anything when I return to England for Christmas. I need to catch up and sharp-ish.

THURSDAY DECEMBER 16TH

It's the big game in the Premier League (Ethiopian PL that is) with Dedebit taking on St George. It's also where we as a squad will be presented to the crowd before the game to take the plaudits for our efforts in Tanzania. It's a nice occasion, particularly for the players for whom this is all relatively new. We all line up on the pitch, receive the handshakes from the dignitaries and more to boot, 7000 Birr per man (£250). Not bad work!

FRIDAY DECEMBER 17TH

Back to the drawing board, and it's more of the same, catching up with my studies whilst keeping an eye on distinctly un-Tanzanian-like weather back in the UK. There is in fact heavy snow, with many of the airports affected. Already my thoughts are turning to my flight back on Monday where by the look of Heathrow airport and its delays and cancellations, I'll be lucky to set off. I definitely don't need that. I love Christmas in England, yes even the cold I'll take. Not sure I could take being stuck in Addis or anywhere else for that matter.

SATURDAY DECEMBER 18TH

Despite the distinct risk of travel chaos, I'm hoping for the situation to resolve itself before Monday. So, I'm going through the motions in many respects. I go to the stadium that day to observe the days' games, but I'm mentally already packing my suitcase. Thankfully, the matches are entertaining enough and I'm even more convinced of the latent talent that exists in Ethiopian football. As a manager, your job is to mould that talent into a team framework. Believe me, that task is made so much easier when the talent already exists. And the crazy thing is, the people here scarcely appreciate the players and their technique. Personally, I'm enthused more than ever about producing a body of work and legacy here, given sufficient time.

SUNDAY DECEMBER 19TH

It's a beautiful morning and with a spring in my step, I walk to church. I can't believe that I've made Wandy take me for so long, when it's only a 15 minute walk at worst. After church I take in another set of games at the stadium before my packing can continue in earnest. Unfortunately, the situation at Heathrow doesn't appear to have eased too much, so I'll be amazed if my journey is anything like straightforward in the morning.

MONDAY DECEMBER 20TH

I make an early start, but I'm right with my prediction and the flight is cancelled until tomorrow morning at the same time. Despite my enthusiasm to return, I take it phlegmatically and even adopt a couple of fellow Brits, Sue and Lesley who have nowhere to go. Not sure what will happen beyond the day, but an invitation to spend a few hours with me at the Sheraton is gratefully received by the ladies and so we all head back. Just as we're getting settled, we get a phone call from the airline, who inform us that they've laid on a flight in TWO hours' time. It all depends upon us getting back to the airport. Can we do it? Yes, we can. Of course we can!

We head back and things go smoothly, until we're ready to board. That's when they drop the bombshell that our luggage won't be with us. Determined to get home, we all raise faint, but ultimately futile protests and board anyway. It's meant to be a direct flight, landing at Heathrow at 9pm. However, halfway into the flight, it's put over the tannoy that we're now heading to Rome. That's where we stay on board a non-moving plane, for THREE hours.

Even worse for Lesley, who's an amateur photographer, a member of the cabin crew has thrown out her precious and expensive film, which she lovingly and painstakingly gathered over the last two weeks. I really feel for her and despite a search through the rubbish, we never find it. There but for the grace of God, go I, methinks! Finally, we set off again for Heathrow, eventually landing in the small hours of a classic English winter. I board a taxi, without my luggage of course, and head for Mark's place in Windsor. I couldn't be happier to be back.

TUESDAY DECEMBER 21ST

Day two of my epic journey involves getting on a train from Windsor to Bristol. And now that the nice people from Ethiopian airlines have my luggage, it's definitely a lighter one! I finally hole up in Bristol late on to find the Christmas lights on and some serious shopping being done. I could have actually started there and then, but I confine myself to a much-needed hat, scarf and gloves combo before heading back to the flat. It's great to see the kids too, although I quickly note the lack of a Christmas tree. That's one more thing to add to the list tomorrow.

I make good on a promise to do an interview for the Daily Express today. Tim Gow is a journalist on the paper and we have a mutual friend, Mark from Windsor. I'm still on a high from the Tanzania trip so we conduct the interview as agreed. It's a far reaching piece all about Ethiopian culture, its football and its people. To any observer, my enthusiasm for all three would be palpable and I'm sure that shines through. At the end he asks for the main challenges coaching there and I highlight the availability of pitches, detailing the incident with Atnafu early in my time there, by way of an amusing anecdote. Little did I know that my comment about the cows on the pitch, would have major repercussions further down the line.

WEDNESDAY DECEMBER 22ND

I wake up and I'm on a mission to do some serious shopping. First up is the tree and after a few surprisingly productive hours, I've had enough for the first day. Nadia and I meet up for the first time since Canada and she informs me that the job specification, in Princeton, wasn't quite as it first seemed. I'm genuinely sorry that it didn't work out for her.

THURSDAY DECEMBER 23RD

Christmas always seems to be a time for reflection and I find myself contemplating the last few weeks. Yes, it's nice to see friends and family and I know how much I miss them in Addis. However, things have definitely got better with the job, six months in and I'm now settled and can see the possibilities ahead and the rich potential. I've harboured a dream ever since going to Ghana in 2008 for the AFCON as a scout for Blackburn Rovers, to one day set up my own foundation/academy in Africa. My current job has certainly opened up that possibility.

FRIDAY DECEMBER 24TH

Last day of Christmas shopping and I'm finally done by the early evening. It's been a mad 72 hours or so and the Onuoras are plentiful enough to cause a big dent in my pocket. My energy levels are down too. Still, it must be worth it because every year for the last few years I've resolved to shop online, but never do preferring the madness of crowds of similarly-minded "lastminute.com"ers.

SATURDAY DECEMBER 25TH

Christmas day!! We wake up, and go to church with Nadia, negotiating the treacherous icy roads and pavements as we go. Later, we head off to London where my sister's cooking Christmas dinner and it's a lovely day surrounded by brothers, sister and nephews. It's late when we arrive back in Bristol, but it's been a good day.

SUNDAY DECEMBER 26TH

Boxing Day, and for me the quiet day, before I head off up North to see the rest of the family. The bad weather has largely done for the Christmas football programme, even if I'd wanted to take in a game which I hadn't, but hopefully the drive will be ok.

MONDAY DECEMBER 27TH

Let the journey begin! I pick up daughter and we head north to Liverpool via Stafford to see my good friend Simon, his wife Michelle and their girls and my goddaughters, Tilly and Lainey. It's been a long time since I've seen them and Michelle, particularly, has had a rough time with her health, so it's good to catch up. We would have stayed longer but the traffic on the roads has been horrendous, so after what seems a short time, we're off up to Liverpool. I drive straight to my Dad's and everyone's there, so it's another nice family occasion, even if the Old Man himself looks increasingly frail with every visit.

TUESDAY DECEMBER 28Th

I get a phone call tonight, having spent another day in Liverpool with family. It seems that someone is finally delivering my luggage to the flat in Bristol, a mere seven days after I landed! Cue some ringing around to see if anyone is home for them to deliver it. Mercifully they are, and crisis over, I've got my stuff back, two days before I'm due to return!

WEDNESDAY DECEMBER 29TH

We head back to Bristol to pick up my son before heading back down to Exeter to see my eldest daughter. Mercifully the traffic's fine and we make good time. My eldest looks great and we all go out to eat. It seems like the perfect end to the holidays to have all my three kids together. We leave for Bristol late on and I have to say goodbye to my youngest, same as I had to with my eldest. It seems my presence in their lives is always just a fleeting one, will it always be this way I wonder?

THURSDAY DECEMBER 30TH

It's the final day in England, but I've plenty to do, before I travel. I'm finally done around early afternoon and I'm under the mistaken belief that time's still on my side. Train delays and a closed station at Reading put paid to that and so it's a mad dash to the airport via train, bus and the ever-priceless Mark and his car. Finally, I'm back where I started 10 days ago, at Heathrow. Only this time I have my luggage and I'm preparing to return to Addis. I'm not sure when my next trip back home will be, it could be quite a while, so at least I can take heart from some good time spent here.

FRIDAY DECEMBER 31ST

It's the last day of what's been a momentous year. I land in Addis on the overnight flight and I'm immediately forking out yet another $20 for another temporary visa. I find the first day or so psychologically challenging, which is perhaps understandable considering the good times I have had over the Christmas period in England. The fact that it's New Year's Eve doesn't worry me too much, it's the fact that I've once again had to leave my family. Nonetheless, it's good to see Wandy and I pick up the money owed to me by the Federation, money that in the absence of my salary, has to last me three weeks. The Sheraton is hosting a spectacular New Year's Eve party and from my room I can see the erected stage and performers including, R Kelly.

To be honest, the significance of the day is less than the date itself, as the opportunity it provides to renew those goals held over from the previous year. I never allow complacency to set in, but I do know that professionally any way, I'm in a far better place now than I was 12 months ago. Sat here alone in my hotel room, waiting to call family back home and with the party in full swing outside, is for now, okay.

SATURDAY JANUARY 1ST

Happy New year! I held out until just about midnight UK time before heading for bed. As per usual, today's not much different from yesterday. I sleep in a little before heading to the stadium to see a couple of the Ethiopian Premier League games and to watch Arsenal beat Birmingham 3-0 on TV.

SUNDAY JANUARY 2ND

The hotel is quiet after the last two nights. I bump into my once next door neighbours on the 1st floor, who I haven't seen for a while. They're Ethiopian born, but only recently returned after many years living in the USA. From that vantage point, it's instructive to hear their thoughts on the psyche of people here which I'm still working out. Like a lot of people they've returned to take advantage of the burgeoning economy here, amidst the rapid economic growth. There's definitely something of the frontier spirit here, you can see it around the hotel lobby where business people meet, swap cards and look to make alliances. It's an exciting time to be in Addis Ababa right now.

MONDAY JANUARY 3RD

All change, there's been an accident involving one of the teams, Adama. A team official plus one of the players has been killed. Wandy and I head to the airport and wait for the sad return of the team. They do eventually return, some four hours after we arrive and it's a heart-breaking affair when they do, with a real out-pouring of grief from everyone present. The media are there, as are the Federation members and several members of the national team, who judging from their reaction, must have known the player well. It's a truly sobering day and football and the Federation suddenly don't seem so important anymore.

TUESDAY JANUARY 4TH

They don't mess about here, the funeral for the team official is taking place today and so Wandy and I head off to Adama to represent the Federation. I always like the drive there and despite the sad occasion, it's nice to get out of the city. We get there early and wait by the house where again, the grief is heart-breaking and very public. We pay our respects as best as possible, including at the burial before heading off to the hospital to visit the still-injured players.

The hospital is small, crowded and chaotic with a small ratio of staff to patients. I marvel at the staff and patients for their sense of calm amidst all of it. I feel more and more humble with every passing day.

I also feel for the players too, who we meet and greet. None of them, thankfully, have sustained life-threatening injuries and I hope that our visit has been of some comfort to them. Not for the first time I'm left thinking, there but for the grace of God, go I.

Before we return to Addis, we take dinner at the hotel in which I stayed back in August. Joining us, is the ex Adama, now Ethiopian Coffee, coach. He's ok, and on the way back it's good to tap into his knowledge and experience of Ethiopian football. In fact my thoughts are that he would make a perfect assistant. Hmmmm…..

WEDNESDAY JANUARY 5TH

I surprise myself today at how conscientious I am with regard to my studies. I've a lot to catch up on and today I get my head down and confine myself to the room. I've no confidence that I'm even going to complete my law course and I've still much work to do, but days like today will definitely help. I take time to make a phone call to the Federation. It's Ethiopian Christmas day on Friday and a public holiday, so I know tomorrow is a must in terms of meeting to discuss our plans for the build-up to the Nigeria game.

THURSDAY JANUARY 6TH

Had another meeting planned for this morning, but it's been cancelled. It gives me a chance to bring myself up to speed with my studies and to rest in the room before our meeting this afternoon. However, it seems that like buses, once one crash happens, another one comes along. This time, thankfully, there are no fatalities involving the Ethiopian Air Force team from Division One. It's another hospital visit though, but this time it's in Addis and the hospital, though hardly modern by UK standards, is several notches up from the one in Adama. Once again we press flesh and offer our best wishes.

After the visit we head back to the Federation and the meeting is constructive, in terms of establishing a process in moving forward towards one or two friendly matches, possibly in February. It's also the first time I've sat down properly with Mr Ashenafi, the new General Secretary. I understand that he's been in the position in the past, which should be a good sign. Less comforting, however, is that he's also not shy to venture an opinion on the team and players too. Could be trouble ahead with him, I muse.

FRIDAY JANUARY 7TH

Christmas day in Ethiopia and it's off to visit Wandy's family. I even try a little of the national dish, Injera, a doughy bread which is a little bitter for my delicate tastes. Actually, it's really nice to see Wandy's mum after all this time in Addis, she looks remarkably strong and handsome-looking and we speak via my pigeon-Ahmaric. After this we go to see Fikru, Wandy's friend, for yet more food and drink. It's a very African thing to go to friends' houses and eat food, and doubly so at Christmas. What I hadn't reckoned on was the insane amount of drink we get through! Fikru and I get through a full bottle of whisky plus several bottles of St George. When we finally left after a few hours, I was seriously steaming and I'm not sure Wandy would have welcomed a breathalyser test right then either. I get back to the Sheraton and instantly fall asleep. A phone call wakes me up and I can't honestly remember the journey home, scary!

SATURDAY JANUARY 8TH

Wake up and it seems that there's an orchestra playing in my head…..loudly! I'm meant to be going to Atnafu's house later which I'm not looking forward to. This seems the perfect excuse to throw in a sickie. When he calls, I feel bad doing so and stick with the plan, much to the chagrin of Wandy who doesn't like Atnafu, and doesn't want to go. I stick to my guns though and we head off.

I get a genuine surprise. It's actually a really enjoyable few hours. His kids are delightful and his wife charming. I get the feeling that he's quite strict as a father and husband, but there's no doubting the love in the household. It certainly rounds out the picture of him. At times, he's been like a two-dimensional villain, despite his evident complexity as a person. Today I have seen the human side of him. When we drink beer and whisky (yes, AGAIN!), I feel relaxed around him for the first time. Even Wandy relaxes though on the drive back it's clear that his views haven't changed. Bless!

SUNDAY JANUARY 9TH

Oh dear, what a heavy weekend it's been! Manage to avoid drink (mostly!) today but the cumulative effect is such that I'm feeling a bit tender!

MONDAY JANUARY 10TH

Time to panic now, as I know my exam and coursework deadline is looming large. I get started on my revision. I do need that smell of fear sometimes, but I wonder if I've bitten off too much this time. I'm probably worse prepared than I was last time if that's possible, so I know I've got to pull out all the stops. Today is the start!

TUESDAY JANUARY 11TH

I'm still waiting for the Federation to sort out my residence permit. They've had my passport now for over a week and I'm never keen to be without it for too long. Later that day, the President calls to say that he's called the media and coaches and I'm to do a presentation in front of them on Friday morning. It only gives me a couple of days' notice and I've got tutorials all this week. Still, it's definitely a good idea to try and be a bit more inclusive with a sceptical media here, so I'm happy to help.

WEDNESDAY JANUARY 12TH

It appears that there's movement on my residence permit. I head off to the Embassy with a letter from the Federation and it seems that the saga could be about to come to an end. However, after an hour surrounded by dozens of others in a similar position, it's clear that it won't be a quick process. I leave some two hours later without said permit. I'm advised it should be available "tomorrow".

THURSDAY JANUARY 13TH

I complete my review of all the games at CECAFA and it's been a good exercise, particularly in being able to analyse both our shortcomings and positives in Tanzania. Once again the talk has been about a lack of fitness all across Ethiopian football, but while this is a factor, it's also a potential red herring. To my mind, if the standards are to rise, there are other factors to address on top of this. I make a mental note to try and drop in issues of facilities and administration. Of course, I will need to do this sensitively.

FRIDAY JANUARY 14TH

The presentation this morning seems to go very well in the end. I do a Power point presentation which is well received and also the Federation do well in organising refreshments and lunch. That sounds simple, but it's the kind of small details that they don't usually do well. So, respect to them for doing it. It's also gone down well amongst the media present and I conclude that it's been a useful and rewarding exercise.

SATURDAY JANUARY 15TH

I wake up early and get back on the study route. There was talk of going out of Addis to watch a game, but a lack of finance put that plan to bed, before it grew legs.

SUNDAY JANUARY 16TH

I wake up and it's another beautiful morning in Addis and I've plenty on my mind with studies etc. I return to the room afterwards and get my head down once again. It looks like the next few weeks are going to be fairly unforgiving in that regard. I speak to Nadia later in the evening and she's on the overnight flight here to Addis. The timing's not ideal because I've got exams looming and I'm way behind, but she starts work at the end of the month so it makes sense to come out now. I'm looking forward to her being here and keep my fingers crossed that it's a good time for both of us.

CHAPTER NINE

Dance Iffy, Dance

MONDAY JANUARY 17TH

Nadia arrives, eventually, after a long flight and as wary as I have been about how we'll get on, I surprise even myself by the extent to which I'm pleased to see her. She seems in good spirits too and we go back to the hotel to relax. We go for a bite to eat and soon she's doing what she does very well, schmoozing and charming all around. Go for it girl!

TUESDAY JANUARY 18TH

Luckily Nadia's acquired some friends in the lobby, so after a morning together, I leave her with them so I can study a bit. My exam and coursework are due in the next week or so and I know that it's important that I finish this course. It may be ok if you're at the very top of the game, but every other coach working in professional football, knows that job security is a pipe dream and you need to prepare for life outside of football. I've probably started this course a few years too late as it is.

WEDNESDAY JANUARY 19TH

I'm off to the Federation this morning where Tim Vine is over from the Premier League to talk about rolling out the Premier Skills initiative, similar to how they have in other African countries. It's soon clear that he and Sahlu, the President, are on slightly different pages as to what they're both looking for. Hopefully, I can help coordinate it. As much as I've grown really fond of the people here, it's also nice to see some people from home and I'm looking forward in two night's time to a reception for them, at the British Council.

THURSDAY JANUARY 20TH

Nadia's still in networking mode so the reception at the British Council will be good for her too in terms of meeting people. It's another change of scene too, as the hotel room is becoming a bit claustrophobic for the two of us.

FRIDAY JANUARY 21ST

The reception is a small, informal affair and it's good for both of us that she's here. She's in her element: charming, warm and intelligent and it's a really enjoyable evening hosted by Barbara Wickham, Head of The British Council in Addis.

SATURDAY JANUARY 22ND

Today begins in less than auspicious style. For the first time since I've met him, Wandy and I are on different pages, time-wise. We're meant to be guests at the Ethiopian Idol talent show and Wandy, yesterday, told me seven o'clock and we were to dress smartly. Naturally, I thought he meant in the evening. I envisaged a relaxing day followed by a night out. More fool me! Seven o'clock, indeed yes, but he meant Ethiopian time which is actually 1pm (they knock 6 hours off European time, when telling the time).

It meant an almighty dash to be there on time. We take up our places in the front row. And that wasn't all, ONE hour we were told, it would last. FIVE AND A HALF hours later, it felt like purgatory. More? Oh yes, it seems they want me to give out certificates on stage for the contestants….and dance! Excuse me? Yes, you heard me, dance! So there I am doing the traditional Ethiopian eskeske dance, in a moment destined for a You tube classic. Please. Lord. Make. It. Stop.

SUNDAY JANUARY 23RD

A mooted plan to go to Awassa is quietly dropped. I'm quite relieved in the end as it would have been a day and a half away from the books. Three and a half hours is a long way after all and thankfully it's about three and a quarter hours further than Nadia can stand to be in a car. So we go out to a Lebanese restaurant to catch some different cuisine than the Sheraton. It's nice too, probably need to get out and eat more than I do. And more importantly, she's happy!

MONDAY JANUARY 24TH

Back to the grind of study after the mini break of the weekend. Thankfully, her friend Elane is back on the scene, so I'm grateful that Nadia has company. I manage to get a bit of work done so later that day, we all head off to Stockholm Bar on Bole Road. It's quite a trendy bar and there is always a good crowd in there. The place is always busy on a Monday night and tonight's no different.

TUESDAY JANUARY 25TH

After a suggestion from the Federation to appease a hostile media, I've selected a B team squad of 17 to begin a two-day training camp at the stadium. There has been no talk as yet of any warm up games despite my several requests. I feel that this, though a good idea in principle, will distract attention from the priority that is the A team. It appears that I'm not alone, when just nine turn up. Apparently there's a re-scheduled game tomorrow involving nine of the players I've called up and no one saw fit to mention it to me until, well, never actually. I've also just found out there's only one goalkeeper too, so I do what I can, but it feels like a monumental waste of time.

WEDNESDAY JANUARY 26TH

The two-day camp has been quietly shelved and I suggest that we try again next week. So, it's another day with my nose in my books, for an exam I'm ill-prepared for. We head off to the Office Bar in the hotel which is always lively with a resident band from the USA. I really can't complain about my living facilities, I wouldn't even dare complain of boredom, for me on my own most of the time, it's just ideal.

THURSDAY JANUARY 27TH

It's the start of the African Union summit here in Addis, and a mass of delegates and state leaders have descended on the hotel. Because of the tense political situations in Tunisia and Egypt, security is even more heightened than it normally would be. In fact, a certain Mr Robert Mugabe of Zimbabwe is staying in the room opposite, which means I have to run the gamut of men in suits with bulges in the jacket, in the corridor outside, when I pick up my room service. I'm very careful not to make too many sharp movements, I can tell you!

FRIDAY JANUARY 28TH
Poor Wandy can't get anywhere near the entrance, so I take the opportunity to walk the 10 minutes or so to the Federation. I know what that sounds like, 10 minutes? I really SHOULD walk that every day. I've provisionally arranged a meeting to resurrect plans for a friendly against someone, anyone, somewhere, anywhere! I'm fobbed off again with some dates and proposed opposition. However, it's only vague talk and with no letters of invitation having been sent, I'm obviously concerned.

With our players, bar one, playing in the local league, friendlies are an absolute necessity more so than perhaps other African players playing in Europe who are exposed to other nationalities and players every week. It's absolutely vital that we play at least one game before we take on the powerful Nigerians. Usually, agents arrange international games between countries and I've tried speaking to David back in London to arrange something. Unfortunately, he's having a hard time getting any real communication with the president with whom I gather he's fallen out with. Oh dear!

SATURDAY JANUARY 29th
Nadia was due to start a job on the 31st of January with the Foreign Office in Whitehall as maternity cover requiring her to be back in England on the 27th. However, it's now been put back a week until the 7th February so there's another week in our claustrophobic room to negotiate.

SUNDAY JANUARY 30TH
I receive the first of many phone calls today. It seems the Ethiopian Idol show aired yesterday, and my "performance", was well-received. It's the big TV show here and widely seen. I'm just quietly praying it's not ended up on You Tube!

MONDAY JANUARY 31ST

It's the last day of the summit and by the afternoon, the hotel seems to be getting back to normal. I inadvertently take an unscheduled two-hour lunch break with Elane and Nadia today too. Two hours! For lunch! Bless the fairer sex, they can seemingly do that at will. I, even without exams looming, can't take 30 minutes without getting restless.

TUESDAY FEBRUARY 1ST

I get a phone call from David offering the tantalising possibility of a friendly match next week in South Africa, all expenses paid. It's a God send and all we have to do is confirm on official headed paper signed by the president and general secretary. I'm excited and get on the phone straightaway, as they need confirmation by tomorrow. Apparently our reputation increased as a result of our exploits in Tanzania, where all the games were televised by Super Sports TV in South Africa. Now, they want to play us. However, if they don't hear from us, they'll play Kenya instead. To anyone it seemed like a win-win situation, money is often an issue, but it would all be paid for. However, there's a problem because Sahlu and David have fallen out and Sahlu's response is lukewarm at best. By the next morning and several phone calls later, it transpires that no letter has been dispatched. I know now that we won't be playing a game this side of the Nigerian match and I might as well get used to it.

WEDNESDAY FEBRUARY 2ND

The mooted "B squad get together" has been put off for another week because there's another midweek game been scheduled. I can't say I'm disappointed, I'm more interested in the A squad of players and many of them are still tied up with club games for another couple of weeks. It would have been different had it been with more numbers, but with barely double figures, it's a pointless exercise.

THURSDAY FEBRUARY 3RD

The Sheik is in town and Nadia goes off to meet him and the family. I can't help feeling that somewhere along the way, I've missed a trick. I wish that I'd managed to meet him very early on here when I arrived, but it's good for Nadia especially if she can firm up some business ideas they've spoken about in the past.

FRIDAY FEBRUARY 4TH

Quiet day today, Nadia has spent plenty of time with the Sheik and his people, which can only be a good thing, I hope. So much so that I barely realise the time, with me starting to claw back some work on my studies.

CHAPTER TEN

Can we please have a game

SATURDAY FEBRUARY 5TH

Time's up and Nadia's returning to England to begin work. It will be good for her and she can do some networking as well as live in London, where she's always wanted to be. It's not been easy and we've not spent too much quality time together. Also, unlike last time she came, it's likely to be June before I'm back in England. It's a sadder departure at the airport than usual.

SUNDAY FEBRUARY 6TH

I'm out for most of the day today, having watched a game in Sebeta, and it's late before I'm back at the hotel. I speak to Nadia who got back to London eventually after her flight was heavily delayed. I've plenty of time to study now, but I'm lacking the willpower today for some reason.

MONDAY FEBRUARY 7TH

Manage to knuckle down and do my work intermittently in the morning before heading off to the stadium to watch the day's games. The guys at the Federation ask after Nadia too, she's clearly made a favourable impression here.

TUESDAY FEBRUARY 8TH

I manage to get to the gym today, a rare event recently and later that evening, I glance at the fixture list over the next two nights -between bits of study- involving 16 African countries. Together with the 16 involved in the CHAN tournament in Sudan right now, Ethiopia is in the minority who don't have a game. When Mr Afework, our Team Leader, calls a little later, I make the point firmly to him. It's not his fault though, he's well-meaning and good company, but it's for the ears of Sahlu who I don't seem to have spoken to for a few weeks now. I hope the message gets through.

WEDNESDAY FEBRUARY 9TH

I wake up and get straight down to my studies. I actually worked well late last night and I get stuck in again this morning. In the afternoon, it's the second chance for the B squad, of whom only nine turned up last time. This time I've invited more players, but still there's the same indifference as only 13 turn up, out of 24. Once more I rip up the session plan for a new one, but make a mental note to let the B squad idea die a slow, painless death.

THURSDAY FEBRUARY 10TH

Meanwhile in a parallel universe somewhere, the Great Naïve Fool that is I, once again attempts to believe that the long mooted friendly match will take place. Of course, I've now shifted my priorities from playing a specific type of opponent i.e. a West African team, to playing any opponent, anywhere at any time. So help me, God! That Nigeria fixture is looming large and Tanzania now seems a long time ago. I'm not fussy, any game will do.

FRIDAY FEBRUARY 11TH

Next week's exam is hovering over me like the Sword of Damocles, as I reflect that this time next week it will be over. It's the thought of exams rather than actually doing them that haunts me. I'm historically not great in exams, always managing to run out of time. Roll on next week!

SATURDAY FEBRUARY 12TH

It's a big day today as Dedebit play a team from Tanzania. The stadium's not quite full, but is in great voice all the same as our heroes put on a five star show. They run out comfortable 3-0 winners, to progress further in the African Champions League. It makes me wistfully think of how the stadium will be when we play there in June.

SUNDAY FEBRUARY 13TH

Wandy turns up around lunchtime and I can't help but laugh when I see him, as he appears to have broken his arm playing football that morning. I'm sure I could and possibly should, have been more sympathetic, but the sight of a driver employing a driver (he's roped in a friend to drive us), is worthy of mire in itself. Sorry Wandy.

At the stadium, it's St George's turn to try and emulate the feats of Dedebit yesterday. Though they start brightly and score, the 2-0 deficit from the first leg is too much to make up and in the second half their attempts become increasingly desperate, before they finally disappear. It's a crushing blow as they're the big hitters of the league and with them perched in mid-table in the actual league, it's a little bit of an expose of their limitations. Even more so, with them contributing several players to the national team, I do hope it's not too much of a psychological body-blow.

MONDAY FEBRUARY 14TH

Valentine's Day comes and goes. It's noticeable that it's quite a big thing, with the flower shop downstairs in the lobby doing some good business. Ah bless!

TUESDAY FEBRUARY 15TH

Studies are getting me down, so I decide on a whim to change the script a little and go out of the hotel for dinner. I find a Chinese restaurant in the lively Bole Road area and the food is as cheap as everything else around here, but perfectly ok. At least it's a change from the room service menu at the Sheraton.

WEDNESDAY FEBRUARY 16TH

I head to the Federation in the afternoon to practically plead for the resurrection of the Friendly game idea to receptive ears. I end up handwriting a letter to send off to Federations throughout Africa, requesting a game. I'm promised that the letter will be typed up and sent off.

That evening I settle down to watch two teams playing football from Planet Beautiful! Yes, its Arsenal v Barcelona and what more could one ask for? It's Arsenal who triumph too, winning the first leg 2-1, only whetting the appetite for the return. It went well at the Federation today so I'm quietly happy, it's been a good day today all round.

THURSDAY FEBRUARY 17TH

One down, one to go! I hand in my coursework today having spent the past few weeks preparing manically. I think it's ok, but I've not done stuff like this since undergraduate days, so it's a bit of a step into the unknown. Tomorrow is exam day, the day after is freedom until more of the same in the summer.

FRIDAY FEBRUARY 18TH

The big day and I can't wait for it to be over. I actually did the online mock last night and was surprised how straightforward it was. It settled any nerves nicely. However, this is MY world we're talking about here and when I arrive at the British Council in the morning, log in on the computer to sit the test, there appears to be a problem. The password given is having none of it and so after a frantic e mail and early morning call to the UK, where it's barely dawn, I leave the building with the test very much, un-sat! Thankfully, when I return, two hours later, I've an e mail and a new password and after 40 minutes of honest toil, it's over. I can now return to normal life. I go back to the Federation to discover that the letter I wrote hasn't been typed as promised and there is no prospect of a game anytime soon. I'm beginning to suspect that it's sabotage on the part of someone whose vested interest is NOT in me or the team doing well in Nigeria.

SATURDAY FEBRUARY 19TH

I wake up and head off to the stadium to watch a game. There are Federation officials there but no-one says anything to me about a game or anything else. I get a strong whiff of competing agendas here. Unfortunately, I don't fully understand.

SUNDAY FEBRUARY 20TH

It's a road trip! Yes, a rare chance of late to get out of Addis. It's a full two hours into our journey before I can relax and take in the beauty of the countryside. The game is in the town of Asala, between Mugher Cement and Ethiopian

Coffee. Coffee, are too strong (get it?) for Mugher despite being the victim of some bizarre refereeing decisions and run out comfortable 3-1 winners.

MONDAY FEBRUARY 21ST

Back on the road this morning, having stayed over in Assalem last night and I'm in reflective mode. It seems to have been a long time since the New Year and already I think Tanzania may have been as good as it gets. If we could have the players for a period of time or play one or two games, then I fancy our chances. Without either…………..

TUESDAY FEBRUARY 22ND

I could do with training a team now, as I'm a bit bored. I guess it's the lot of an international coach as opposed to club coaches, but I should have coached some of the smaller sides a bit more than I have. It is something I would do differently if I could start again. I did one or two sessions before Christmas and it was good for both them and I. But I've probably got bogged down with other stuff since then. I promise to make time to do it again.

WEDNESDAY FEBRUARY 23RD

Bingo! The Women's team coach has approached me and asked me to do a coaching session right on cue. They have some Olympic qualifying games coming up and are due to play Ghana at the national stadium in a few weeks' time. I accept. I'm glad to make myself useful.

THURSDAY FEBRUARY 24TH

It's turning out to be a strange week this one. I haven't lost my enthusiasm for the job, nor have I ever once felt anything other than being blessed for the opportunity. My feelings alone have been enough to sustain me even though I've a nagging sense that I'll not be in the job for too much longer. I know I'm popular amongst ordinary people, largely due to Tanzania, but I'm not sure in terms of the long term whether that will be enough somehow.

FRIDAY FEBRUARY 25TH

Chat to Nadia today and it's clear that she's enjoying her new surroundings in London. It sounds like she's right in the middle of the West End and making friends. Not sure she's enjoying the job too much, but she's a true London-phile so I'm happy for her.

SATURDAY FEBRUARY 26TH

Two games today at the stadium and though it involves the smaller clubs, there's always at least one interesting player, to make a mental note of. Later I check on the results from back in England and notice that my old gaffer Peter Taylor is to leave Bradford City, paving the way for a return to management for my good friend, Peter Jackson. I spoke to him and he's delighted and I am for him despite my high regard for Peter Taylor too. Ah, it's a cruel business football management and none crueller than in England right now. Yeah I'm better off where I am.

SUNDAY FEBRUARY 27TH

I decide to have a real chillaxin day today and so I head off to the pool area for the first time in months. With a good book, I Pod and wine on tap, it's a picture perfect Sunday afternoon. Later on, I watch Arsenal lose the Carling Cup final to Birmingham, a result that depresses half of Addis Ababa in the process.

MONDAY FEBRUARY 28TH

A late night last night meant no chance for an early gym session, so catch up with some paperwork, before heading down to a quite productive day at the Federation. The ordinary staff there are lovely, always very warm and welcoming and as I'm picking up more and more of the language, we can even chat and at times, exchange, banter.

TUESDAY MARCH 1ST

Today's the 9th anniversary of my late Mum's death from cancer and with the game in Nigeria only a few weeks away, I imagine that she's looking down with maybe a bit of pride. The Boy's done good! I take the opportunity to ring my Aunty, in the USA, and we have a good chat. She's even promised to support Ethiopia in the upcoming game!

WEDNESDAY MARCH 2ND

Oh for simple pleasures, a simple day coaching the Women's team at the stadium. They've a great enthusiasm and it's nice to be out on the field again. On the whole, they speak better English than the guys so a combination of that, plus my increasing understanding of Ahmaric means that communication is fine. That helps as I'm terrible with names and it takes me ages to remember them. There are some good players amongst them too and I think they really enjoyed the session, much as I did.

THURSDAY MARCH 3RD

Almost out of the blue, I get a phone call promising a game in Ghana a week before the Nigeria game. Leaving aside the logistics of travel etc, it could be the perfect preparation. The odds of the game going ahead, are probably still only 50-50, but I'll take that right now. Yesterday, there was no prospect.

FRIDAY MARCH 4TH

There is definitely a spring in my step now, as I make plans for the squad to meet on Monday. I meet at the Federation and the discussion enough is an improvement on what has previously gone on, or not as the case has been.

SATURDAY MARCH 5TH

I'm just on my way to see the big game between Dedebit and Ethiopian Coffee, when I bump into Sahlu at the Sheraton. Now, we've barely spoken a word in the last few weeks, almost certainly as a consequence of his now sour relations with David in London over some unrelated issues. I think it was the reason why he didn't sanction the Friendly game against South Africa last month. Sadly, the only losers were the players and of course, me. At least he reassures me that the Ghana game is a real possibility. So, that's a consolation.

SUNDAY MARCH 6TH

It's the first day of training tomorrow so I spend the day preparing my sessions for the week. I know how tough an assignment it will be and I can't leave any stone unturned in my preparation.

MONDAY MARCH 7TH

So, the first day's training and it's like the first day at school, or at least it would be if school opening times were flexible. WTF??? Out of 23 players called up, six are on time, 10 are late and seven don't show at all. Talk about a let-down. I end up preaching to the largely converted about time keeping (again!) and discipline in general. I'd forgotten about this never-ending battle every time we gather. If the past is a guide, it will take the best part of a week before they're fully on board.

Nevertheless, it's a start of sorts and when I return to the Sheraton that evening, I'm quietly satisfied. Unlike the staff at the Sheraton where the lights are out and the storm of earlier appears to have wreaked a little mayhem. So much so, that it's a bit of the Blitz mentality with everyone downstairs in the bar, surrounded by torches and being guided to their bedrooms by lamps.

TUESDAY MARCH 8TH

Day Two and yesterday's absentees have shown up, belatedly. I resist the chance to admonish them further, because we simply have no time to lose. I think I called that right, particularly as they're key players, whose performance levels raise the standards appreciably. By now I'm back in the old routine of meeting the players in the evening for dinner at their hotel. It enables me to keep an eye on them individually and as a group, and vice versa. It's bang in the city centre too, so a good test to see if there's any sneaking out at night. Not that I'd know of course, but hopefully they don't know that!

WEDNESDAY MARCH 9TH

We train in the morning today and to break up the week, we do a gym circuit followed by a few lively games of basketball. My motto is that even when the guys are working physically hard, you can always make it fun. Judging by the loud noises coming from each and every one of them, I think they enjoyed it.

In fact the only downside is still the time-keeping as the gym session is a good hour later than scheduled.

THURSDAY MARCH 10TH

I make sure I work the guys hard today. The quality's good again in training, but I'm aware of players who haven't played many games and those who arrived late, so we finish training with some interval running which judging by their faces, they weren't expecting. They certainly don't appreciate it! I play my trump card though, promising them a night out on Sunday to see the famous Ethiopian singer, Helen Berhe. It does the trick, the smiles have returned!

FRIDAY MARCH 11TH

Those pesky Nigerians have named their squad and it's a roll call of players playing in some of Europe's biggest clubs. I tackle the issue head on revealing the players' names and clubs. I then remind them of the Nigerian's vulnerabilities and urge the "respect, not fear" mantra.

SATURDAY MARCH 12TH

Training today is a full scale 11-a-side match. I play what I would consider as a first X1 against a second X1. Predictably enough it's the 2nd X1, who are leading at half time, so a little tweaking of the line-up for the second half, leaves me a lot happier by the end. The game ends 1-1. Though there's still some selection headaches and overall work to be done, I'm not too unhappy after the first week. More of a problem is the prospect of the Ghana game now being in jeopardy due to a problem between the route from Accra to Abuja. Also despite the proposed game being only a week before the main game, they're refusing to sanction an additional two players to take with me. I think it's fair to say that the prospects are no longer looking good.

SUNDAY MARCH 13TH

A day off for the players today and for Yours Truly, who's got some serious studying to catch up with. I get a bit done, but time comes around quickly and before I know it, we're all off to see the Helen Berhe concert. She's a popular and well known singer here and I must confess, not without a little charm!

When she finally appears after a warm up act or several (!), she's warmly received by the crowd. And that really should have been that, but not here. There then follows what looks like an awards ceremony which was news to me, followed by a two hour romantic comedy film. I was hoping to be back at an early time, but here I was a full FIVE hours later sat in the same high school issue chair, craning to see, but inwardly craving sleep. At least you couldn't complain of the lack of value for money!

MONDAY MARCH 14TH
Start of the second week and there's a good feel to the squad. Training's sharp and bright and the players are working well. We're still awaiting the arrival of our key striker, Fikru, from South Africa and two other players who have stayed with their club ahead of an African Champions' League game in Cairo next weekend. But that triumvirate apart, they're working well under close inspection.

TUESDAY MARCH 15TH
More of the same, as the days seem to be flying by. I've mentally pulled the plug on a friendly match in Ghana. It's too much of a risk and the hassle of flying over the extra guys, two days after, would create too many problems. As much as we could have done with the game, I'm sure that it's the right decision and I confirm this to the Federation. I can tell they're secretly delighted at the saving of money, but it's still the right call, I believe.

CHAPTER ELEVEN

The beginning of the end

WEDNESDAY MARCH 16TH

Straight to the gym this morning and we spend a quick hour with the guys, doing weights and playing basketball. I was planning to get some work in, but a potential nightmare scenario is unfolding that means I have to go to the Federation. I've just been notified that my sending off to the stand in the Madagascar game in October, means I'm banned from the technical area for the Nigeria game. It's the worst possible news and puts a cloud over me for the rest of the day. Of course, I'm going to challenge it, but the reality is that I'm potentially stuffed. I write a letter to CAF, but I know I have to really prepare this team like never before if we're to get anything out of the game.

THURSDAY MARCH 17TH

I'm resigned to my fate re the Nigeria game, but I intend to go on the offensive as soon as I get the inevitable confirmation. It will be good fuel for the fire. Only a select number of people know and that's the way it will stay, certainly until we get over there. We train in the morning, as in the afternoon there's a game between Eepco and Adama. One of our players is playing for Eepco and though his work rate and attitude are exemplary, I know he's the antithesis of an Ethiopian midfield player, possibly because of those two reasons. I'm a hostage to criticism if I select him and we lose, so the easy option would be not to take him. That said, he's unquestionably worthy of a place in the squad.

FRIDAY MARCH 18TH

I shelve my plans to do some defensive work today, in place of a small-sided game instead. It's always a better response as players enjoy them more and besides, I'd rather do the defensive work and let them absorb it, over the weekend. It's been a long week and I'm flagging by the afternoon, so by the time the evening comes, it's a deserved glass of wine or two. The Nigerian media have started getting a little more voluble about the game, far more so than the media here who so far, have been conspicuous by their absence.

SATURDAY MARCH 19TH

We begin training and get through some defensive work which we'll need to do well in Abuja. Later we go to watch Arsenal draw 2-2 with WBA whilst Man Utd beat Bolton 1-0 with a late goal, perhaps a defining game in the title race.

SUNDAY MARCH 20TH

This time next week I'll wake up on the morning of the game, but unlike the week that's gone, I'm feeling positive about the whole experience. Preparation is right on course and so long as the week ahead pans out as expected, we'll be as prepared as we possibly can be. I could ask no more of myself and others. It's a sunny morning too, in contrast to the week before, and when my phone goes off in church (on vibrate, no worries), I merely shift it to my cardigan pocket without much thought. But then disaster strikes! In a feat of cunning and a sleight of hand that I don't recall, someone steals the admittedly visible phone and my plans for the day are all about to change. It later transpires through broken English that four guys were seen "brushing" past me and let me tell you they were that good, I don't even remember passing them.

MONDAY MARCH 21ST

Back training today and still no sign of the Dedebit guys, Mengistu and Daniel. I later hear that rather than report to the hotel, they stayed at their own houses. Not a good start and perhaps a sign of things to come. In the meantime we enjoy a light session ahead of a game tonight against a local team from Division One. As for the game itself, it was a useful exercise and run out for the guys. For me, it confirmed my thoughts on the goalkeeping issue: one of them could catch a high ball and the other couldn't. Simple!

TUESDAY MARCH 22ND

Our final session, before we leave, is a light one, as I attempt to keep the spirits high. Besides, most of my anticipated starting line-up played a minimum of 60 minutes last night. We have our now customary send off, the night before, from the president at the hotel and it's now that I start to feel the full weight of responsibility on my shoulders again. With competitive games few and far between and the last one back in December, it all starts to feel brand new again. I'm ready though, bring on the Naija's!

WEDNESDAY MARCH 23RD

Early start for the airport and predictably enough, we leave late as some of the players are late again. Though we've left plenty of time in the schedule, this is a recurring theme and though I'm trying my best to let things pass, it becomes increasingly difficult to ignore.

I'm wearing my now 15-year-old shirt that my mum bought me one Christmas. It's a tighter squeeze now than it was then, but it reminds me of her. On the flight to Nigeria, I sit next to Fikru. He's a good guy and a big player for us, but it's the first time I've sat down for any real length of time to chat about him and his background. Naturally confident, he's good company and the flight passes pleasantly. It's nice to touch down back in Nigeria after a five-year absence. Abuja is less manic than Lagos, thankfully. We go for a walk after we've checked in to our hotel and everyone seems happy and relaxed.

THURSDAY MARCH 24TH

The first morning at the hotel and the curse of Atnafu strikes again! What is it about travelling abroad that makes him so idle? He's already asked permission to travel to Lagos in lieu of some treatment for his daughter tomorrow, a two hour flight. It's always a hard one because family comes first and his daughter's a lovely kid, but sweet baby Jesus, we're not here on holiday! I reluctantly allow him to travel after training, so long as he's back late the next day. He then plays his joker. Myself, and Mr Afework are off shopping to pick up some necessary provisions for the players and in lieu of tomorrow's absence, I ask Atnafu to accompany us. He hangs around just long enough for the Doctor to take the last place in the car, pretending vainly with palms outstretched that he would have loved to come, but there's no room in the car. Honest guv'. It seems after a four month absence, its déjà vu all over again.

FRIDAY MARCH 25TH

Atnafu hasn't travelled to Lagos in the end it transpires and after his "performance" yesterday, I don't bother asking him why. However, when he's late to the lobby along with half the players, my patience is done. In a display of frankly, excellent controlled aggression, I lambast him for both his time keeping and yesterday's shenanigans. All he offers is his usual, "yes, right you are", like it's the first time it's ever occurred to him that he might help buy stuff and be punctual. After all, he is the assistant coach, and all that. Talk about high maintenance!

SATURDAY MARCH 26TH

The guys are late again despite me speaking to them all. I've had to turn a blind eye to some of it, otherwise you can drive yourself crazy, but here when we have to train at certain times and be reliant on police escorts etc, it's not good enough. I let them have it with both barrels in a fairly breathless tour de force of controlled fury. The day had started badly when I received confirmation that I will be banned from the technical area tomorrow night. It hangs over me for most of the morning. Nonetheless, the blast was justified in its own right and it does have the desired effect. Training is both sharp and aggressive, it seems like it might have been the best thing to dispel a nagging feeling of lethargy around the camp. There may well be a lack of belief here, but the restless energy of Tanzania and even Madagascar, seems to be missing, and this, unwittingly, could have been just the tonic needed to restore it. As the night draws in and I contemplate what tomorrow might bring, I'm restless and sleep poorly.

SUNDAY MARCH 27TH

I make arrangements for a taxi and as per my usual ritual, I'm off to church. And what a joyous affair it is, full of colour music and majesty around the congregation. Back at the hotel and time-keeping is immaculately observed for meals and meetings before we depart for the ground.

The national stadium is modern and impressive, similar to the one we encountered in Tanzania. An expectant crowd has already gathered and I know, by speaking with the local media, we're not expected to pose the Super Eagles too many problems.

On the pitch, before the game, I set out my cones ready for the warm up, only to find out that I won't be allowed on the pitch at all. That leaves Atnafu to take it and I stay in the dressing room unable to even watch from the distance of the tunnel area. I give my last words of encouragement and advice, including the immortal and time-honoured phrase, "keep it tight for the first 20 minutes and we'll be fine".

So, when we're a goal down inside 40 seconds, it's fair to say that my advice has fallen on deaf/nervous/terrified ears. Oh well, at least I can reorganise from the bench, oh wait, hang on…..

We hang on until half time, with the score still 1-0 and I attempt to re-organise as the dressing room appears to fill up with Embassy officials and all manner of uninvited guests. No matter, I issue fresh instructions and the guys leave the dressing room with words of encouragement in their ears.

We have our most encouraging spell of the game as we finally get our passing game going and the home crowd goes quiet. However, they have a trump card still to play: WBA's in-form striker Peter Odemwingie comes on after an hour and starts to wreak havoc. Nigeria make it two and then three in quick succession, followed by a fourth right on the stroke of full time. My attempt to defend the players by pointing to the difference between Premier League players like John Obi Mikel, Peter Odemwingie etc, and my squad, leads to mirth in the press conference as it's misinterpreted as being a joke at our expense. It's not and never was meant to be, but it's part of a process whereby the light seems to be dimming perceptibly now, on my Great Adventure. It's been a chastening experience and I'm naturally deflated.

MONDAY MARCH 28TH

Wake up early and though I'm not ready to ring the Samaritans just yet, the heavy sense of defeat still hangs in the air. It was the manner of the defeat really, only four or five of the team really did themselves justice and I hadn't managed to instil in them a sense of belief, something I always felt was a strength of mine. Had I been too defensive as well? I'd set us up to defend with depth and play on the counter-attack, but had this sent out the wrong message? At least in the last game in Tanzania we'd gone down with glory, this felt like we'd not really turned up. It was much harder to take.

On the flight back, I sit on my own, deep in my own thoughts. I reflect on the preparation, tactics, players and staff. The sober reflection is that we've come up short. We arrive back to a muted reception, certainly compared to when we returned from Tanzania, but at least the president shows up. I later learn that my Daily Express interview from back in December has been syndicated. The headline of 'Cows on the Pitch' has not gone down well.

CHAPTER TWELVE

They think it's all over... it is now

TUESDAY MARCH 29TH

I'm tired after last night's arrival and sleep well. However, I wake up with the nagging feeling that I could be playing out the dying embers of my time here. The reaction to the defeat has been one of largely weary resignation.

However, the game itself is no longer the front page headline and even I can understand the gist of the Ahmaric radio debate on the coach having to use his own money to buy boots for the players. The Daily Express article is now the only debate in the media right now and there's a storm brewing.

WEDNESDAY MARCH 30TH

Still no official word, save for an emergency meeting of the committee planned for tomorrow. Here, no news is not necessarily good news. My "death" should it come, is likely to be slow and painful rather than swift. Death by a thousand cuts, as Ken Bates once described it, talking about Claudio Ranieri's sacking by Chelsea back in the day. At least he had a big payoff to get by on, no guarantees with me.

The bright future contemplated only a few weeks ago, now looks dark and gloomy again. I feel rootless again and I'm desperately missing my friends and family. Who else would come out here alone? I must be mad, better off in England, I tell myself. Yeah right, to do what exactly? There weren't many jobs of any description last time I looked, never mind in football. All I can do is finish my studies and contemplate my fate.

THURSDAY MARCH 31ST

The sound of silence is now deafening. No word yet from anyone and it feels a little like when I was dismissed at Swindon back in 2005. We'd been relegated the week before and for the next four days, I received no word from anyone in the club, even with regard to planning for pre-season which was barely four weeks away. When the end came it was furtive, sneaky and then finally, brutal in its execution. So, I'm sadder, older and wiser now and mentally steeling myself for whatever's in the pipeline. I busy myself as best I can, but I can guess what's coming.

FRIDAY APRIL 1ST

It's my son's birthday and I ring him early to wish him the best. It's just another reason why my return back home can't come soon enough. I'm missing them all a lot right now. I put down the phone and it's not long after that I finally get the call from Sahlu. It's a rambling chat in broken English, but I finally get the picture that I'm to appear before a committee (disciplinary?) next Monday. I can understand the concern over the paper's headlines, but I can't understand the length of time it's taken to get here, given that it's been all over the news. But at least I'm in the picture now and later, when I pick up my letter confirming the meeting, I'm relieved to find out that there's no mention of any disciplinary aspect to it. From a legal point of view, that's important. I've already got my arguments in place, so it's looking a bit better on that front.

SATURDAY APRIL 2ND

Wandy and I head off to watch a game at Sebeta before heading back to the National Stadium for the second game that day. It's my first real outing all week and people I speak to are largely polite and sympathetic. I'm heartened by that enough to feel a little happier until some kid shouts, "4-0", at me. Cheers!

SUNDAY APRIL 3RD

Another day and I've been told that my presence has been politely requested at the Federation in the morning. Hmm, interesting times ahead then. The rest of the day is spent in nervous anticipation. The meeting could and probably will determine my future out here. I sleepwalk through another forgettable game at the stadium before heading back to the room to prepare.

I check the article from the Daily Express with some dismay, it's definitely been "sexed up" and it's not even got Tim Gow's name to it. It's also factually incorrect as it says that we had to clear cows off the pitch before we trained. Not only was that NOT the case, but I never said it. It's a small point, but I know things like that are hard to read from proud people like the Ethiopians and I have a lot of sympathy for that. It certainly lacks even a sense of the enthusiasm and regard I had for my adopted country, not the finest piece of journalism I've ever come across I conclude, but I've got take a measure of responsibility for allowing the heady glow of Tanzania cloud my judgement, in even mentioning it.

MONDAY APRIL 4TH

D-Day! I'm surprised how nervous I am when I wake up, like it's an interview or exam. I take breakfast, but the butterflies are definitely there as Wandy picks me up. A nervous wait then ensues, whilst Mr Afework arrives late. Soon, the meeting is in full swing. I thing I find the right blend between honesty, regret and defiance. It's a fair hearing all in all, the only time I think it gets a little rude for my liking is when someone asks me to "tell us about yourself, a little about your background". I nearly choke on my incredulity! It's like I've been called to an interview with people I've not met before, not so-called colleagues, most of whom I've known since the day I arrived here. Even if it was impossible to do their own homework, the tone is a little disrespectful I feel, but I let it slide. Afterwards I reflect on the meeting and conclude that it's gone as well as I could have hoped for. The rest is up to them.

TUESDAY APRIL 5TH

I'm trying to put all the shenanigans behind me now, because I've got that assignment to hand in and I've got to focus. I slip effortlessly into exam mode which basically consists of me forgetting to take in such basics as food and water, never mind picking up the phone. It's four o'clock in the afternoon before I emerge, blinking into the sunlight; 3,000 words written, but still another 1,000 to go.

I convince myself that I've worked hard enough for now and relax for a few hours to take in the Real Madrid v Spurs game in the Champions League. Spurs lose Peter Crouch, sent off after 10 minutes and the tie is virtually over then, as Madrid put four goals past them. The next day the papers are critical of the manager, similar to when Arsenal were similarly blown away against Barcelona. I've got to wonder what planet these people are on? With 11v11, it's actually a contest of sorts, but against teams of that calibre, with 10 men, you've no chance! How is that possibly the fault of the coach and his tactics......he said, speaking as a paid up member of the coaching fraternity!

WEDNESDAY APRIL 6TH

An early start, so I'm up at the crack of dawn, with the deadline at 2pm (BST) that day. I'm speeding along nicely, comfortably cracking the 4,000 word limit. It's now in need of some editing. Some careful pruning later, I get there, with, wait for it, ONE word to spare. It's fair to say that I'm now feeling very pleased with myself.

I meet up with the Wand-meister and I'm in better spirits than him when his beloved Chelsea are deservedly beaten by Man United in the remaining Champions League quarter final. Ah bless, at least I've finished my assignment.

THURSDAY APRIL 7TH

Still positive in thought and deed now that the Sword of Damocles' Assignment is no longer hovering over my head, I positively skip to the stadium to take in the first of two games played in the afternoon. Halfway during the second half I'm quietly told that my presence is requested at the Sheraton for a meeting that evening. It's something of a shock and I begin to fear the worst. Don't ask me what happened in the remainder of the game, I simply haven't got a clue. I hasten to suggest that my mind was elsewhere.

My thoughts are confirmed when I arrive in the lobby to be greeted by the President, Vice President and Federation stooge. It's entirely predictable what is said, a few platitudes followed by the big hit, that they want to release me from my contract. Apparently the newspaper article has been a little inflammatory for them and though privately I get that bit, I also feel it was the smoking gun needed by some to get rid of me.

I wish I knew who exactly, and this is perfect fodder for conspiracy theories, but the simple truth is that this is football politics and I was in the midst of it from day one. I've been caught between some who wanted a different approach to tap into the football culture here and help improve the country's standing with a foreign coach, and the traditionalists who believed amongst other things that footballers shouldn't worry about physical fitness, but be mere ball players in the tradition of a country once described in football terms as the "Brazilians of Africa". Throw in some vested interest and a power struggle near the top and you're close to the nub of the matter.

I quietly listened before going into impassive mode explaining that I've a TWO year contract, not one as they've suggested and will be speaking to "my people" in England to arrange my settlement. No, I didn't really know what that meant either, I just hoped it may carry some weight when it came to a bargaining position. It didn't.

On the one hand, I'm genuinely sad, because despite my obvious frustrations, I love the job and the potential of it. I know it'll be a long time, if ever, until I find myself in the same position again. I tell Wandy who I know is upset too, but we content ourselves with a beer or two before each of us leaves the other to our thoughts.

FRIDAY APRIL 8TH

The morning after yesterday's bombshell and I'm fluctuating between looking forward to going home and of course, an uncertain future. There's a game this afternoon which ordinarily I would go to, but for now I'm staying away from all things to do with football. Until everything's resolved, it's best, I think. I haven't said anything to anybody else yet either, I'll just wait for now.

SATURDAY APRIL 9TH

I decide that my study hiatus should really come to an end and resolve to catch up on missed lectures. I surprise myself on my powers of concentration (interspersed with me watching my boys, Everton dismantle Wolves 3-0, in the early kick off). Before long, it's off to watch the results from England.

SUNDAY APRIL 10TH

I resolved yesterday, in the face of more negative press, that today would be the start of the fight back. After all, my fate here is sealed anyway and it's only the terms of my leaving that are in dispute. So, it's about time I put the record straight re that article. I appear on a friend, Samson's, Afro FM show in the morning and make my case. There will be bigger audiences to convince, but it's a start and I'm not finished yet, same again tomorrow.

MONDAY APRIL 11TH

So, potentially another week of impasse stretching out ahead of me, as I wait to see what all the talk between the Federation and David in London brings. My first exam is only five weeks away now and I've yet to find the requisite concentration to settle down and contemplate "the Law", when my future is so up in the air. I hope it all gets resolved properly now, it's getting lonely again here now.

TUESDAY APRIL 12TH

My Skype account and David's phone bill are taking a bit of a battering as he keeps me updated with what's happening. In truth he could just have said "Nothing" and left it at that, such is the progress, or lack of it. I'm quite relaxed though and decide to hold out for a decent settlement no matter how long it takes. I'm now almost exclusively confined to the hotel room.

THURSDAY APRIL 14TH

There's a garden party at the British Embassy this afternoon to celebrate the Queen's birthday and Mr Afework from the Federation calls to say he'll meet me at the hotel and we can travel together. No problem, he's one of the good guys and when he declares himself to be there to negotiate a settlement too, I'm all ears. When I'm told what it is, I'm distinctly underwhelmed and unimpressed. I make my feelings known. We resolve to meet again in the morning and Wandy drives us both to the Embassy.

It's a nice afternoon, a slice of the Home Counties on the Embassy grounds, as along with about 500 others, I enjoy the hospitality and warm sunshine. We stay for a couple of hours, rubbing shoulders with mostly diplomats and staff from various embassies in Addis and I manage to catch a quick word with the ambassador Norman Laing, who I've met before. He is a very congenial host. I was also searching out Barbara Wickham from the British Council, mindful that my dispute with the Federation could take a turn for the worse, but she's not present today, so I keep my counsel.

"Oh my prophetic soul", the Bard himself once wrote. Wandy calls me later in the evening a little distressed, the car and his services have as of tonight been withdrawn. I'm now transport-less and him jobless. When he comes to the hotel, he's sorry for me and I'm sorry for him. It looks like my earlier fears have been realised.

FRIDAY APRIL 15TH

Mr Afework comes by again this morning as scheduled and I point out that I'm less than impressed with the Federation's new negotiating stance, not least because it's a breach of my contract. He says that he wasn't aware of it and I'm minded to believe him. Less believable however, is that he's come back with the same offer as yesterday (minus the car makes it a REDUCED offer relatively) and this time hints at citing "disciplinary" measures as reasons for dismissal. He also suggests that my accommodation provision would be withdrawn.

I weigh up my options and decide they're not great. I'm in a foreign country and attempting to negotiate a settlement with people effectively ready to throw me out of the hotel if I don't sign the settlement in front of me. What's more, they have already taken the car and driver from me. It's starting to resemble a scene from The Godfather, if I return to my room, there may even be a horse's head on my pillow! A few hours and several phone calls later, I reluctantly conclude that I've taken this as far as possible here and that they're not for budging. There's another route to go down with FIFA, but right now, I need to get out of here. I sign the settlement letter whilst laughing off their scarcely credible insistence on a "send-off" party for me. Is it April Fools' Day? They seem genuinely shocked that I don't want one and offer to provide me with my car and driver again. You couldn't make this up!

SATURDAY APRIL 16TH

So, I'm playing out the last few days of my time here and whereas a week ago I'd have given anything to be still here back in my job, I now can't wait to go back home. This weekend will be a form of Purgatory, waiting for the flight on Monday morning. I speak to a few journalists, one of whom told me that my contract had been terminated for disciplinary reasons. Uh oh, here we go, cue the mud-slinging. I resolve to speak to as many journalists as possible, but only to speak positively of my time here. Class and dignity always triumph over a war of words. Later that afternoon, I meet up with Atnafu for a coffee and it's the first he's heard of it. He is shocked and disappointed, but not surprised given his knowledge of the politics here. He's essentially a good guy if unbelievably frustrating at times and after our initial difficulties, I've grown to like him. We chat warmly about the past 10 months, whilst contemplating an uncertain future.

SUNDAY APRIL 17TH

By a drip-drip of information, the news has seeped out and the media are now all over the story. I'm determined to enjoy my last day here with as many of the friends I've made. I keep it light, positive and refuse to fire bullets in any direction.

The evening's a little emotional as a few of the players and friends come and meet up for a drink at the Ras Hotel in town. My phone picks the wrong day to mess up, but I'm aware that a lot of people have sent messages of support via those who've been able to show up at such late notice. It's fine, I make a little speech thanking them all for coming and then one by one they leave. Atnafu and I share a warm and tearful embrace as do three of the players who have managed to be here.

MONDAY APRIL 18TH

I'm taking an early flight and I'm happy to go along with just Wandy to the airport. Bertokan the journalist who travelled with us says she'll be at the airport and that's fine, she's a nice lady. However, when Sahlu rings to say that he'll be there too, I'm not too impressed. I think he could have done more, not least with that friendly game back in February. Even though I know it wasn't his decision, that's not much comfort right now.

He's accompanied by Mr Afework and another guy from the Federation whose name I always forget, but who is actually a decent guy too. I checked my bags before returning to join them all for a coffee. We all share an occasional awkward silence deep in our own thoughts on our exclusive island of stillness, whilst all around us was the flurry of activity as the airport buzzed with movement and noise.

Sahlu has bought me a book all about Ethiopia, the irony of giving me it as I'm leaving, not being lost on me. Still, it was a nice gesture and I warmed to him again, as I always had done. It's an awkward embrace between us and I say goodbye to all, except Wandy.

He's been like a brother to me out here these last 11 months and as I look at the clock, I realise it's time to go. I don't like goodbyes, at the best if times, and this is the hardest of all. We share a warm embrace and the 'Big Guy' sheds a tear, as I do. I walk off and steal a quick glance back. He's inconsolable and once again, it sets me off.

The plane's on time, and I take my seat. We taxi along the runway and set off without fanfare. The adventure is over.

Over the next week or so, I'm told there was a bit of a storm of protest at the Federation, as no one had been given any valid reasons for my departure. Stepping into the void, they've cited some "issues" which has only served to deepen the mystery. In short, people aren't having any of it and are demanding answers. I even got wind from David that they were considering re-instating me. Really!!

I know enough to understand that these things eventually blow over given time and by the time Nigeria arrived on Addis at the beginning of June, there was a new Belgian coach and they gained a creditable 2-2 draw though he and Atnafu didn't get on apparently, and the latter was sacked shortly after his arrival. The new coach then followed him out of the door after five months, which put my length of term in greater perspective, and the team now has a local man in charge. I wish them well, and I'll always follow their fortunes closely and look out for their results.

EPILOGUE

A year or two down the line and I still keep in touch with a few players via Skype and Facebook. Wandy, after a few months of no work and no money, finally joined his wife and son in New York and I plan to go and visit him one day soon.

The sharp-witted amongst you would have worked out that some of the Premier League results are now TWO seasons old and it's true that it's now over TWO years since I left Addis with many deep and life-affirming memories. In fact, what's truly remarkable is that I barely recognise the tense, stressed guy back then.

Yes, the frustration at times was palpable and Atnafu, for example, would have tested the patience of Job. That said, I'd like to think that I'd handle him and other situations a lot differently if they happened now.

When the dust had settled on the whole episode, what stayed with me was how much it had humbled me. If this reads like a critique of Ethiopia, its football and its people, then I've failed pretty miserably at telling the story I wanted to tell. I've no hard feelings towards anyone there. I felt and still feel that I was privileged to be the country's coach and in actual fact, felt a deep and lasting regard for one of the oldest peoples on God's Earth. Their beauty, pride and spirit, an everlasting source of joy and inspiration.

And whilst my circumstances are very different now, not being a full time coach with all its attendant stresses, the last couple of years haven't been without challenges, in a number of different ways.

Aside from some part time work for which I'm eternally grateful to the Premier League, I was out of work for a full year with savings long gone and hope and optimism under attack. Even from my own, "glass half full" perspective, that was a tough time.

What sustained me was the enormously rewarding periodic visits back to Africa to deliver coaching courses for the Premier League, where I was fortunate to spend time in Senegal and Nigeria, up skilling the domestic coaches there around good practice and their community projects based on Health and Education. It not only gave me my fix of football, but a job of significance and worth.

Also my father passed away in March last year after a long illness, coinciding with the 10th anniversary of my wonderful late mother's passing. They were the last link to that generation that came to England in search of new beginnings, and I still marvel at my Mum, especially who raised her five kids single-handedly on a diet of Faith, Love and sheer force of will. I remain thankful to them for the sacrifices they made for me and my siblings. I hope to see them again in the next lifetime.

Nadia and I went our separate ways soon after I returned, and we didn't have any contact for a long time. More recently though we met up on good terms and over a bite to eat, could reflect fondly on our time together. She's an occasionally formidable, but deep down very sweet girl with a heart of gold, she's a good catch for somebody.

So what now for me? Well, after some time out of football in August last year, I started working full time for the Players Union, the Professional Footballers Association. I work in the Coaching department delivering Level 2 qualifications, and also have responsibilities for Equalities. Given all the issues involved in football over the last couple of years, it's that side of my work that promises to engage most of my time, moving forward.

So, there you have it, we're up to date, and where things go from here is anyone's guess. It was the great American comedian and film director Woody Allen who once opined, "If you want to make God laugh, tell him about your plans for the future". I'll second that.

"In his Heart a Man plans a course, but the Lord determines His steps"
Proverbs 16 Verse 9

ND - #0328 - 270225 - C0 - 234/156/9 - PB - 9781780912332 - Gloss Lamination